VOLUME III ● EASTER

AN ENCOUNTER

A DAILY DISCOVERY IN DIVINE WORD

VOLUME III ◉ EASTER

An Encounter

A DAILY DISCOVERY IN DIVINE WORD

MAURICE NKEM EMELU

Bien
Cleveland, OH

Nihil Obstat   Fr. John Opara, Ph.D.

Imprimatur   Most Rev. Dr. Augustine T. Ukwuoma
                    Bishop of the Catholic Diocese of Orlu
                    24th May 2021

Published by
Bien LLC | Cleveland, OH

Publisher's Cataloging-in-Publication Data
Emelu, Maurice Nkem.

Published in Africa by Paulines Publications Africa

An encounter : a daily discovery in divine word. Volume Three: Easter, Years A, B, & C / Maurice Nkem Emelu. – Cleveland, OH : Bien LLC, 2021.

p. ; cm.

Summary: An encounter is a book of rich prayerful conversation and reflections, for personal and group faith sharing. Meditative, educational and didactic, most of the contents are religious sentiments of a heart in love with God. Each of the individual reflections has one central message to inspire the reader for a more profound sentiment of encounter with God. In the process, the person's discovery journey will deepen.

ISBN13: 978-0-9601097-2-2

1. Faith--Biblical teaching. 2. Prayer--Biblical teaching.
3. Catholic Church--Doctrines. I. Title.

BS680.F27 E44 2021
234.23--dc23

Project coordination by Jenkins Group, Inc. | www.jenkinsgroupinc.com

Front cover design by T. Dewayne Johnson
Interior design by Brooke Camfield

Printed in the United States of America
25 24 23 22 21 • 5 4 3 2 1

Dedication

In loving memory of Most Reverend Dr. Gregory O. Ochiagha, the pioneer bishop of the Catholic Diocese of Orlu, Nigeria, who courageously bore the pains of sickness with the hope of resurrection until the Lord called him home on December 29, 2020.

To Father Christopher Ihenetu and the sisters of the Immaculate Heart Congregation who were assigned as Bishop Ochiagha's caretakers for their exceptional and compassionate care during the moments of his journey to eternal rest.

And to the sick and dying—for courage.

CONTENTS

ACKNOWLEDGMENTS

*T*hanks to thousands of audiences who read the first draft of these reflections as a daily blog on the Gratia Vobis Ministries' website and various social media. Their regular feedback and request for book versions helped me fine-tune the ideas that resulted in these organized volumes. I am most grateful to Jeanne Curran, my adopted mom, for proofreading the volumes. Father John Opara, Ph.D., a liturgist, carefully reviewed these contents in the light of liturgical theological appreciation. Immeasurable appreciation to my Bishop, Most Reverend Augustine Ukwuoma, Ph.D., for the Imprimatur and constant inspiration. Thanks to my dad, Alphaeus Emelu and family, who have always been a source of strength.

INTRODUCTION

*G*race to you, my dear readers and friends!

I invite you for a daily prayerful walk with God's Word in the form of a personal reflection based on Catholic Scripture readings for Easter season. As I noted in the first volume, I wrote most of the reflections before the Blessed Sacrament. Before the Lord, I found the serenity and peace of soul that inspired more profound prayerful sentiments within me. I began to dialogue with God's words. Often those words flowed as I gazed at Jesus exposed in the Sacrament, seeing his strength and his glory. I was drawn to contemplate the holy face of Jesus as he looked at me from the center of his love in the most Blessed Sacrament.

I wrote these words as prayerful conversations. Some of the contents are meditative. Others are educational or, if you will, didactic. Most are religious sentiments of a heart in love with God. Each reflection is written in a simple style fit for a general audience. Drawing from biblical information read in the light of the Catholic Church's understanding, they are personal reflections for spiritual nourishment. I approached them using an audience-driven communication method in the light of applied theology. The style is heavily narrative and reflective without ignoring logical applications. Thus, these reflections are not a systematic study of any given subject. They address various themes with the goal of effectively applying faith-based ideas to today's realities.

The goal for these daily reflections is to be a spiritual companion in daily life. Call them a boost for the day or a spiritual companionship for everyday life. In simple terms, they reflect an encounter and a discovery. Each of the sixty-eight individual reflections has one central message geared toward inspiring the reader to more profound sentiments and encounters with God. Accompanying each reflection are reflective questions and targeted prayers for personal growth.

These daily reflections are empowering words accompanying readers on the journey of life as they continue to discover the gentle Word of God. They reflect the journey of a soul in love with God who is trying to meditate on God's Word in the silence of his blessed presence. Alone with God, the soul hears those words the noisy world often silences.

The primary audience for these reflections is people seeking to deepen their spiritual lives. They could be teens, young adults, or adults who want a resource that can serve as a daily nugget in their relationship with God and one another. Thus, this work consists of personal and group inspirational and faith-based readings. It may serve the needs of ordained and lay ministers who are looking for resources to prepare their talks, sermons, or exhortations, but this isn't the primary objective. I also wrote to provide families and small prayer groups with talking points to engage with in their weekly, bi-weekly, or monthly Bible sharing. I envisage a situation where small groups in churches and faith-based organizations may use the content to customize their personal prayerful exchanges.

This particular volume draws from the readings of the Easter season. With a minimum of one reflection and a maximum of four for each day, I trust the average reader will have sufficient themes to engage with in prayerful dialogue. A personal reflective guide and prayer conclude each reflection. Serving as specific but suggestive guides, they will help readers extend the conversation by adapting it to their unique situations.

Towards the end of this volume, I include a Pentecost novena guide focused primarily on the traditional gifts of the Holy Spirit as a substitute for the reflections. I hope this prayer guide will help any individual or group engage more effectively during the Pentecost novena period.

God love you. God bless you.
Father Maurice Emelu, Ph.D.

How to Use This Guide

*R*eaders may approach this work in chronological order or glance at a piece from any of the themes in the way they deem convenient. However, my suggestion is to read the appropriate reflection(s) for the stated day. In that case, readers will meditate on the particular theme(s) as their spiritual companion for that day. Followed in this manner, it will take approximately forty-seven days to go through the entire sixty-nine reflections. For group study, I recommend assigning individual members of the group a topic from a particular week or month of focus. Then each person can lead the group to reflect deeply on their assigned topic. The reflect section plus the prayer that conclude each reflection are helpful in this process. The Pentecost novena is a prayer guide centered on the traditional gifts of the Holy Spirit plus other charisms of the Spirit. You may find it helpful during the Pentecost novena season.

WEEK ONE OF EASTER

Brief Summary of Main Themes in the Ten Scripture Readings for the Easter Vigil

Readings: Genesis 1:1–22; Genesis 22:1–18; Exodus 14:15–15:1; Isaiah 54:5–14; Isaiah 55:1–11; Baruch 3:9–15, 32–4:4; Ezekiel 36:16–17a, 18–28; Romans 6:3–11

Reading for Sunday, Year A: Matthew 28:1–10

Reading for Sunday, Year B: Mark 16:1–7

Reading for Sunday, Year C: Luke 24:1–12

*T*he first reading of Genesis (1:1–22) is the story of creation and divine blessing for creation: "God saw all that he had created, and it was very good."

The second reading of Genesis (22:1–18) is the call of Abraham and his epoch-making testimony of faith in response to God's call and request.

The third Scripture reading (Exodus 14:15–15:1) is the story of God's deliverance of Israel through the leadership of Moses. The deliverance is a typology of the ultimate salvation of God's people through the Lamb of God, Christ the Lord.

The fourth reading (Isaiah 54:5–14) describes God's marriage with his people and the tender and everlasting love of God for us, his chosen people. It prophesizes the future of God's people, the New Israel, and how they will be solidly established in divine peace.

The fifth reading (Isaiah 55:1–11) is a divine invitation to all who are thirsty to come to the renewing, everlasting Covenant of God.

Reading six (Baruch 3:9–15, 32–4:4) is a clarion call to repentance and acceptance of wisdom, which is from God, already a pointer to the Divine Logos (Christ), the splendor of God.

The seventh reading (Ezekiel 36:16–17a, 18–28) reveals God's word to Prophet Ezekiel. It highlights how God will sprinkle clean water, the water of regeneration—a typology of baptism—upon us so we can be clean. Baptism in Christ makes us a new creation, bearing new hearts. "I will create a new heart in you" refers to the seed of eternal life (sanctifying grace).

These seven readings from the Old Testament point to the new life in Christ that Easter brings about. Easter is the apex of the Paschal mystery, the rallying point of all we do and celebrate as believers.

The next two readings are from the Epistles and the Gospels.

Reading eight (Romans 6:3–11) testifies to the Resurrection and how Christ, who rose from the dead, lives forever, and how they who believe in Christ will rise from the dead too and live forever. On Earth, being dead to sin, we live for righteousness. Thanks be to the grace of Jesus Christ.

Matthew 28:1–10 describes the first witnesses of the Resurrection. According to this particular synoptic gospel, among the witnesses are Mary Magdalene; Mary, the mother of James; Salome; and the testimonial of an angel who reassures them of the Resurrection. This passage also portrays how, as they run to proclaim "He has risen" to the disciples, Jesus appears, reassuring them, "Do not be afraid. Go tell my brothers to go to Galilee, and there they will see me" (Matthew 28:10).

Mark 16:1–7 confirms that the day after Sabbath, "Mary Magdalene, and Mary the mother of James, and Salome, bought spices, so that they might go and anoint Jesus." It was the Lord's Day, the first day of the Week, a tradition which has been part of the inspiration for why the Church embraced Sunday as the Day of the Lord. The women's exceptional love for the Lord is shown. They become the first witnesses to go and announce to Peter and the other disciples that the Lord has risen and will meet them in Galilee.

Luke 24:1–12 adds to the eye-witnesses' account of the resurrection, the unbelief of the apostles. It notes how Mary Magdalene and Jo-anna and Mary the mother of James and the other women testify to the apostles what they saw and heard from "two men . . . in dazzling apparel" that the Lord has risen. It shows the apostles' unbelief since "these words seemed to them an idle tale, and they did not believe them" and Peter's commitment to run to the tomb and see for himself.

Easter Sunday of the Resurrection

Alleluia! Death Is Not the End of the Story!

*Readings: Acts 10:34A, 37–43; Colossians 3:1–4
or 1 Corinthians 5:6b–8; John 20:1–9*

*T*he story of our Lord Jesus's suffering and death on Good Friday appears to be the story of the triumph of falsehood over truth, injustice over justice, and evil over goodness. The Lord was falsely charged with crimes he did not commit. He was unjustly sentenced to a death he did not deserve.

Good Friday shows us how agents of evil can collaborate to work against the truth and righteousness. Herod and Pilate, old enemies, unite in a bid to fight the truth (see Luke 23:12). Nations and cultures that were never on the same page become allies. Barabbas, a known rebel and criminal to the Roman authorities, is set free, whereas Jesus Christ is criminalized (Matthew 27:15–26; Mark 15:6–15; Luke 23:13–25; John 18: 39–40).

Politics and religion become one so that Jesus may die. Even at the grave, a combined military force of two troops who have never been on talking terms work as perfect allies to guarantee the dead Jesus (whom they call an impostor) does not resurrect. What more? The devil must have formed its spiritual prison for the Son of God, Jesus.

The worst of the plot is betrayal. The Lord's good friends betray him. His trusted companions desert him, and his closest associates deny him. The people he loves demand his crucifixion and choose to have the bandit Barabbas released in his place. It is a story of betrayal and lies, dishonesty and meanness, unfaithfulness and wicked violence directed against an innocent and seemingly helpless victim.

Good Friday is the apex of institutionalized evil. It embodies the worst of evil in the world. If that were the end of the story, it would have been a terrible chapter in history. Glory be to God, it wasn't and isn't.

Death is not the end of the story. There is one more enduring chapter. It's the most important chapter because, as the saying goes, they who laugh last laugh best. In the last chapter of the story of Jesus' earthly life, we see him rise from the dead in glory and majesty. He is vindicated. His enemies are shamed and confused. Jesus regains his eternal glory with the Father. He is the Lord who prevails over all humankind, his enemies included. For us, his followers, this is Good News, a cause for us to rejoice and be glad. This is, therefore, the day the Lord has made, let us rejoice and be glad (see Psalms 118:24).

Why must we rejoice? We rejoice because our faith in Christ has been vindicated (see 1 Corinthians 15:16–17). Truth triumphs over falsehood. Justice wins over injustice. And tragedy becomes a redemptive comedy.

It's like watching Superman. You see an innocent and helpless victim being attacked, robbed, kidnapped, assaulted, and tortured by a wicked assailant. You feel sad at the triumph of the bad guy. Then, almost at the point of desperation, when the victim is about to surrender to the despicable treachery of death, down from the skies comes Superman to the rescue. He battles and defeats the bad guy and rescues the innocent victim. You feel happy at the triumph of justice, the triumph of truth.

It is good news to know that Truth is immortal. Some people suppress Truth, accuse it of being a lie, condemn it, torture it, kill it, and even bury it in the grave, but be confident of this: on the third day, Truth will rise again. Truth lives. Those who hold on to Truth live on too.

Society may institutionalize lies. Some create for themselves a standard of "righteousness" that is a matter of convenience. People may even build moral and religious norms based on the god of their hands. Yet someday there will be an Easter morning. Easter, therefore, is hope for us in our daily commitment to the Truth. Remember this and do not give up on Truth even when everybody else seems to surrender. Easter inspires us not to give up on justice and not to give up on doing what is right.

Truth will always be the truth even when the world around us calls it a lie. We must learn to believe in the sun even when it is not shining, knowing that, by and by, it will shine again. This isn't simply a whimsical wish, as one philosopher argues. It is a metaphor of the power of faith in God, who is the light of the world, the eternal sunshine. We are to rejoice and be glad.

Rejoice and be glad even when you are going through tough times. When you pass through betrayal, unjust discrimination, lies, and misrepresentations, rejoice. When the economy is in terrible shape or when the enemy seems to be winning the battle in your life, be confident.

Christ has won. We know that in Christ, we shall win too. Someday, we shall have our Easter Sunday. Hallelujah! Praise the Lord! Happy Easter!

Reflect

How does the message of Easter speak to me as a believer? Do I believe that the Resurrection assures me that I will have life in abundance? How does this promise reassure me in my life struggles?

Pray

Lord, you assure us through the words of your servant Saint Paul that if we die with you, we will reign with you. You rose to reassure me that I will rise from the hubris of my falls. May I treasure the message of the Resurrection in my heart and be inspired by it. Amen.

Monday within the Octave of Easter

Do Not Be Afraid

Readings: Act 2:14, 22–23; Matthew 28:8–15

Welcome to day two of a fifty-day celebration of the joy and celebration of the Resurrection. Did you know that Saint Athanasius called the fifty days from Easter Sunday to Pentecost Sunday "Great Sunday"? One could say that every day of the fifty days is celebrated like one great Sunday of joy, happiness, and rejoicing in the risen Lord.

On this day two of our "Great Sunday," may we reflect on the first greeting of the Resurrection, "Do not be afraid" (Matthew 28:5, 10).

In February 2016, a terrible earthquake shook virtually every house in Kern County, California. I was living in California at the time and was in my living room studying when it seemed the whole house was about to collapse. I became afraid, but I remembered God's words: "Do not be afraid." These words held renewed meaning for me that day. Amidst the immediate danger of the possibility of the earthquake causing the house to crumble, I found I could rely on my faith to keep my composure.

Many things we hang on to lose their relevance when catastrophe strikes. If nothing else, the coronavirus pandemic of 2020 has taught us this much: the power of God's Word means a lot to fearful people, especially when we are dealing with fear of the unknown.

Are you sometimes worried that something terrible or terrifying may happen to you or your loved ones? Is your deteriorating health a source of concern? Do you fear it could be a symptom of a terminal health condition such as cancer? Are you afraid your sudden fever or cough could be the dreaded COVID-19 or another deadly disease? Do you fear your life savings will vanish or that you may lose something precious to you? Do you fear the unknown? This is a monstrous feeling that keeps many from a joyful life.

Fear of the spiritual kind is the worst of all. It might be called the fear of fear itself. Many are tormented by something they can't quite fathom. They might not be aware that the object of their concern is fear itself.

Here is good news to tuck in your heart: the victory of the Resurrection wins over fears of all kinds. The Lord wins. So do those who walk and live in the light of the of risen Lord.

The first witnesses of the Resurrection according to Matthew 28, Mary, the Mother of Cleopas, and the other Mary, are afraid when they come to the tomb of Jesus. But the angels they see tell them, "Do not be afraid" (Matthew 28:5). Similarly, later that same day, the risen Lord speaks to them and to the disciples, reassuring them, "Do not be afraid" (Matthew 28:10).

In the resurrected Lord, our Savior Jesus Christ, our fears are swallowed up in victory. The worst of our fears is the fear of death and all that goes with it. Some of these fears include the realization that we will leave behind our dreams, material treasures, and many things we hold dear. It is worse if we sense those assets will be inherited by people we do not much admire. For some, this is challenging. However, for the children of the Resurrection, this fear is conquered completely. We know nothing matters except eternal peace.

God reassures you and me: "Do not be afraid. I am with you and will save you."

How about passing this message on to someone near you or someone who needs it the most: "Do not be afraid. The risen Lord wins."

REFLECT

What are my greatest fears? Am I brave enough to pause for a while and reflect on them? What mechanism do I have to handle my fear? What role can my faith in the risen Lord play to assure me?

PRAY

Lord Jesus, let the power of your Resurrection save me from unholy fears and attachments. Amen.

Tuesday within the Octave of Easter

Resurrection—Mary Magdalene, the Women, and the Rolled Stone

Readings: Acts 2:36–41; John 20:11–18

*E*ver wonder why of all the followers of the Lord Jesus, Mary Magdalene is singled out by Saint John as the first witness of the Resurrection?

Scripture notes, "Now on the first day of the week, Mary Magdalene came to the tomb early, while it was still dark, and saw that the stone had been taken away from the tomb" (John 20:1).

This instance and the verses that follow are the first of eleven appearances of the Lord Jesus to his disciples between Easter Sunday and Ascension Thursday. The Lord appears to individuals and groups. Once, he appears to a crowd of about five hundred. The Lord's resurrection is a fact, not a hallucination.

The Synoptic writers, namely Matthew, Mark, and Luke, suggest the number of women varied from two to four. However, Mary Magdalene's name is consistent in all four Gospels as the first witness of the Resurrection.

The women go to the tomb. The Gospels of Mark 16:1 and Luke 24:1 explain they go to anoint the body of Jesus. This rite is a Jewish practice. It is a kind and holy gesture in honor of the dead. They can't do it the night before because it is the Sabbath. The women, including Mary Magdalene, an incredible believer in Jesus, are devout Jews who never want to defile the Law of the Sabbath. However, their love for Jesus cannot be stifled by death.

Nothing indicates the women believe Jesus will resurrect. They, like the apostles, do not believe this. They merely want to anoint their dead Lord and bring closure to the sad event; so, no sooner is it dawn than they journey to the tomb. What they see is a surprise: the large stone rolled over the tomb of Jesus has already been removed. This is the first miraculous sight of the Resurrection.

The Gospel of Mark gives a peculiar context to the women's worries as they go to the tomb: "Who will roll away the stone for us from the door of the tomb?" (Mark 16:3). Indeed, during the most despairing moments of their lives, many ask, "Who will roll the stone?" and "From where shall my help come?" Mary Magdalene, along with the other women, is worried.

Easter is a permanent reminder that the stone has been rolled away so we can see the empty tomb. Never again will our hope be interred. The stone no longer sits upon the tomb in our life. It is by the Lord's Resurrection that this has been done. It is marvelous in our eyes.

Earlier, a massive stone covering Lazarus' tomb at Cana is rolled away by the command of the Savior Jesus Christ. The same Lord and Savior doesn't want a stone laid upon the miracle of the Resurrection. The angels roll the stone at his behest, for God will not allow his loved ones— Mary Magdalene and you and I—to miss the fact that inside the tomb, a new hope has dawned—Resurrection.

Rejoice, you believers in the Resurrection. Christ lives.

REFLECT

Do disappointments, suffering, or even the death of a loved one make me lose faith in God's saving power? What can I learn from the kind of love and commitment Mary Magdalene shows the Lord even when he is still in the grave? How strong is my love for the Lord?

PRAY

Lord, I know and believe that nothing can separate me from your love—not death, fear, suffering, or persecution. Give me the grace of affectionate loyalty. Amen.

Wednesday within the Octave of Easter

Resurrection—the Way to Emmaus

Readings: Acts 3:1–10; Luke 24:13–35

*T*oday's reflection draws a lesson from the Lord's appearance to the two people on the way to Emmaus (Luke 24:13–35), inspiring us to overcome fear and despair.

Cleopas and the other disciple, whose name is not provided, are on their way to Emmaus. One might say they are victims of fear, despair, and anxiety. They must have been in shock, skeptical about the news they've heard of the risen Lord. Their journey to Emmaus happens the same day the women break the news of the empty tomb. Recall that the apostles and other disciples dismiss the report, thinking it is nonsense or gossip (see Luke 24:11).

Perhaps they are still struggling with disappointment that the person they expected to be the Messiah is an impostor. Many of the earliest disciples did not believe Christ could be crucified. They thought the Messiah could not be killed. These two on the road to Emmaus feel that all the "pious baloney" claiming Jesus has risen must end. Their enthusiasm about the Messiah in the person of Jesus has petered out. They likely simply want to return to their old ways of life.

On the way to Emmaus, they cannot help but engage with their worst fears, namely, the events surrounding the death of Jesus and the seemingly false report of his Resurrection. The scene is a prototype of the despair that grips many people in life whose hopes have been devastated.

The weapon of despair that brandishes the image of the empty tomb does not allow its victims to see why the tomb is empty. It grips its victims with unfounded fear and, like a wild cat feasting on its prey, will not let go. It tries to create another world of its own, and with a touch of mimicry, projects its world as real. Its imposing impersonation is so loud and daring that it takes the likes of the Biblical David to surmount its Goliath-like posturing.

Despair is a demon against holiness, the life of virtue, and the life of faith. It is a definite obstacle to grace and opportunities. It impedes the will to succeed.

The two on the way to Emmaus have been lured into the living room of despair. They can only be let out by the help of the prince of hope, the silent listener to every conversation. The risen Lord has to clear the doubts, refresh the minds, and gladden the hearts of these two, so he joins them on the way to Emmaus and calmly listens to their frustrations.

The Lord listens with an utter sense of pity. These two people, like the other disciples, are of little faith. They despair.

Along the road to Emmaus, Jesus speaks the Word to the despairing Cleopas and his companion. At that, they feel a fire within their souls. This fire is the power of God that dissolves fear, doubt, weakness, and sin and inspires people to faith. "Faith," Scripture says, "comes by hearing." Without the message, nothing could be heard (see Romans 10:17–18).

But this kind of knowledge of God and the power that comes with it can be deepened. Though the Lord may be like a silent guest in our midst, he reveals himself more and more. Full recognition of the risen Lord goes deeper, from the spoken and written Word to the breaking of bread in the Eucharist.

> **REFLECT**
> From time to time, I am tempted to despair. I feel that God is distant from me. I wish Jesus could appear physically to me and show me the way. I wish I could see him as often as I want in my moments of loneliness and despair. I get frustrated knowing this is wishing and asking for too much, but the Lord is with me already, especially in the Eucharist. How strong is my devotion to the Eucharist and to Christ's word in Scripture?
>
> **PRAY**
> Lord, give me the grace of renewed love for you in the Most Blessed Sacrament, the Eucharist. Increase my devotion and love of you in the Word and the Sacrament. May this reassure me of your abiding love and presence. Amen.

Thursday within the Octave of Easter

Fifth Appearance to the Disciples

Readings: Acts 3:11–26; Luke 24:35–48

We come to the Lord Jesus' fifth appearance (Luke 24:35–48), his appearance to the apostles and a few others with them in Jerusalem, as proof of his Resurrection. Recall that the Lord's first appearance is to Mary Magdalene (John 20:11–18). The second is to the other women visiting the tomb (Matthew 28:1f; Mark 16:1f). The third is to the two on the way to Emmaus (Luke 24:1f). The fourth is his appearance to Simon Peter (Luke 24:34).

It's important to note that among the worst doubters of the Resurrection are the disciples of Jesus, chief of whom are the apostles. I love how Venerable Fulton J. Sheen describes the apostles' skepticism: "The skeptics of yesterday, namely the apostles, were worse than the skeptics of today."

Sometimes this aspect of their initial doubt toward the possibility of the Resurrection is forgotten. Some argue that the disciples expect the Resurrection. Others suggest the Resurrection is the fruit of their hallucination, having wanted and desired it so badly. These arguments aren't consistent with the reports documented in Scripture about what happened.

Scripture chronicles the mood of the disciples when the two on their way to Emmaus break the news of the possible Resurrection of the Lord to them and Jesus suddenly appears:

As they were saying this, Jesus himself stood among them and said to them, "Peace to you." But they were startled and frightened, and supposed that they saw a spirit." And he said to them, "Why are you troubled, and why do questionings rise in your hearts? See my hands and my feet, that it is I myself; handle me, and see; for a spirit has no flesh and bones as you see that I have" (Luke 24:36–39).

No better story shows the disbelief of the apostles and disciples. Their doubts are deep, their fear beyond measure. They believe Jesus is dead. They know he died. They saw the soldiers pierce his side, the sword go straight to his heart, and blood and water gush out. They witnessed him take his last breath. In particular, John the beloved was present along with the other women, including Mary, the mother of the Lord.

The disciples are sorrow stricken. They know Joseph of Arimathea rolled the stone over Jesus' tomb. They are not to come close for fear the guards who keep watch over the grave to prevent fraud will arrest them. Terrified, their hopes are shattered, their dreams aborted. Jesus is dead.

Therefore, they are beside themselves to hear rumors of a Resurrection. For many of them, and for many today, it is a fairy tale.

Again, the disbelievers of yesterday are far more hardened than those of today.

Jesus' fifth appearance and the actions he undertakes demonstrate he lives. He makes some specific gestures and carries out some grace-filling actions to reawaken their faith. These include his word of peace (his usual greeting), addressing their doubts, and showing them his pierced hands and feet. They also include his call for them to touch him and eating bread with them. These go-the-extra-mile efforts prove he isn't a ghost. He is alive!

My friends, no matter the doubts you may have about the Lord and Resurrection, the facts speak for themselves. Allow the risen Lord to open your eyes to see more. Do not doubt.

REFLECT

When doubts about one aspect or another of my faith creep in, how do I respond? How do I feel at these moments? Am I afraid of losing something precious? Am I anxious? Uncertain? How do I manage that fear and turn it around to become a gift back to God? Do I believe that, even in those moments, God demonstrates his abiding love?

PRAY

Open my eyes, Lord, to see and believe in the power of the Resurrection. May it be reassuring when I am in my dark moments of life. Amen.

Friday within the Octave of Easter

Jesus' Appearance to Seven Disciples by the Sea

Readings: Acts 4:1–12: John 21:1–14

I continue reflecting on the theme of the Lord's Resurrection.

As I have shown previously, there are several biblical proofs to justify the Lord's Resurrection. The Lord's appearances aren't mere random occurrences. They aren't a phantom or a product of hallucination or mere ghost appearances, as some skeptics claim. There is a touch of order and strategy to them. The way and manner in which the Lord appears, not just to one or two people but to many, should be convincing to the average person.

The risen Lord appears to many, from individuals to hundreds of people, more than eleven times. The appearances to seven of the disciples by the Sea of Tiberias (John 21:1–14) is significant. Pay attention to the details.

Simon and the other disciples go fishing. They aren't daydreaming or praying in the Upper Room, nor are they deranged people. They know precisely their left hand from their right.

The death of Jesus is a deep blow, for sure. The hoped-for Messiah is dead. Hence, following the call of Simon, all seven return to their old profession—fishing. They are fishermen.

Then comes the appearance of Jesus by the Sea of Tiberias and vivid proof of the Resurrection. This third appearance to the disciples takes place at a named location and fulfills the five "Ws" and one "H" of any valid eyewitness account. Who was involved? (The seven disciples.) What happened? (Jesus appears.) Where does it occur? (By the Sea of Tiberias?) When? (It was morning because the Jewish fishermen at the time of Jesus fished in the morning.) Why does this happen? (To prove Jesus truly resurrected in bodily form, not as a ghost or a spirit.)

The "How" is evident from the opening line in the Gospel of John 21: "After this Jesus revealed himself again to the disciples by the Sea of Tiberias; and he revealed himself in this way" (John 21:1).

The evidence of Christ's post-resurrection appearance by the Sea of Tiberias is so striking that the writer of the Gospel of John cannot skip even the most minute details. We learn the names of the disciples: Simon, Thomas, Nathaniel, James, and John, the sons of Zebedee. Only two of the seven names are not mentioned. We learn details about Jesus standing on the beach. We hear little about the disciples' inability to recognize the Lord even after he starts a friendly conversation with them, asking, "Children, have you any fish?" (John 21:5). We hear details about Jesus asking them to cast the net at a particular side of the sea and how they make a huge catch.

If these eyewitness accounts are a hallucination, it is an unbelievable one. Also, such an illusion taking over the minds of seven fishers on a boat on the sea would be beyond human experience.

How about the big catch and John's sudden realization when he confesses, "It is the Lord"? What about the details of the charcoal fire with fish lying on it and bread already prepared by Jesus? What about Jesus having breakfast with them? Do ghosts eat breakfast?

These are proofs beyond the imagination of the apostles. They know it is impossible for the dead to appear in bodily form, yet they see Jesus. They touch him. They hear him ask them to cast the net in the sea. They eat with him. This kind of phenomenon is the complete opposite of what they could have imagined, yet they see it right there and touch the body of the Lord.

The truth is, Jesus has risen and is alive. He is the Lord.

REFLECT

If someone were to ask me why I believe in the Lord Jesus as my Lord and Savior, would I have my answers ready? If I were asked why I am a Christian, would I have answers? Am I passionate about my faith? Am I glad to share my testimony? What personal testimonies do I have that show my connection with my faith?

PRAY

Lord Jesus, let me know you, the risen Lord. May I continue to love you with all my heart by the power of your grace. May I never waver in my love for you. Make me infectiously passionate about my faith in you as Lord and in your Church as your body. Increase the power of personal witnessing in my heart. Amen.

Alternative Reflection

The Power of Witness

Readings: Acts 4:1–12: John 21:1–14

I share how a personal experience of the Lord's healing grace strengthens the power of bearing witness to the faith. I use it as a source of inspiration to you in your daily commitments and passion as a believer in the Lord and Savior, Jesus Christ.

Over the years, I've known many people who have encountered the Lord in a personal way. I've met and interacted with people to whom the Lord has shown the favor of a miracle. Sometimes it was a healing miracle. Sometimes it was a miracle of providence. Sometimes it was a miracle of conversion. You name it.

In my life and ministry, I've seen the Lord Jesus Christ do wonders. He heals the sick. He dispels the darkness of evil. He overturns satanic strongholds. He heals and renews broken relationships. He strengthens the weary. The Lord goes on doing incredible things. For anyone the Lord has touched in a personal way, there is profound joy. There is also the boldness of singing the hallelujah of his greatness.

One notices that the faith of those the Lord has touched deeply and personally is more robust. They are more passionate. They aren't apologetic for believing in the Savior Jesus Christ. They aren't shy about their faith. Good, bad, and ugly experiences do not make them waver. Not even the wounded body of Christ and Church scandals make them lose faith. They've seen. They've witnessed good things. They've sipped the Water of Life. Their testimony is reliable and profoundly personal. They know that in good times and bad, the Lord of hosts is their strength and their refuge.

Yes, miracles are signs. They are needed signs when faith grows cold. They are needed signs when we pass through a dark night experience capable of tearing our hearts apart. In such moments, we look up to the Lord, from whom comes our help (see Psalms 124:8).

Be assured of this: the Lord hears. The Lord works miracles. The Lord intervenes. Those divine interventions strengthen the power of bearing witness to the faith.

When we witness the Lord's miracles, we are bold to proclaim them. We learn from basic catechesis that we have to encounter the transforming grace of the Lord to be a witness of it to others.

The beautiful and bold testimony of Saint Peter as recorded in Acts 4:1–12 is proof. The Lord has used him to heal a disabled person at the Beautiful Gate (see Acts 3). The once timid Peter is no longer afraid to tell what he has seen. Peter has seen the healing power of God in a personal way. He can't keep from declaring what he has seen. Not doing so would harm his core and moral sense.

Peter declares, without mincing words, it is ". . . by the name of Jesus Christ of Nazareth, whom you crucified, whom God raised from the dead, by him, this man is standing before you well. This is the stone which was rejected by you builders, but which has become the head of the corner. And there is salvation in no one else, for there is no other name under heaven given among men by which we must be saved" (Acts 4:10–12).

REFLECT
What personal testimonies do I have that reconfirm my faith in the Lord Jesus as Savior? Am I willing to share this testimony with others?

PRAY
Lord, make me more aware of your great miracles in my life and the lives of those around me. May my life be a testimony of your incredible miracles. I also pray for the grace of boldness of faith in telling others about your great works. Amen.

Saturday within the Octave of Easter

The Bold and the Guilt Stricken— Resurrection Lifts Them Both

Readings: Acts 4:13–21; Mark 16:9–15

The Gospel of Mark gives further details of the Resurrection arranged in a condensed but chronological form typical of Mark's Greek style. At least twelve proofs are presented in one chapter (see Mark 16). They include the evidence of the women at the tomb, the rolled stone, the angel's conversation, and the missing body of Jesus. They also include Jesus' visit to Peter, the fear of the women who report to Peter what they see, and the consistent doubt of the disciples. Finally, they include the appearance of Jesus to Mary Magdalene and the two disciples out in the country (Emmaus) and the Great Commissioning of the disciples as the central mandate of the Resurrection.

Imagine being one of the disciples or apostles of Jesus. Imagine being Peter or John, the beloved. Imagine that, during the arrest and crucifixion, you run away lest you be arrested or killed like Jesus.

Three days after Jesus is killed, say you hear rumors the crucified Jesus is resurrected and alive. Some women you know pretty well say they saw him. They say he spoke to them and would like to see you and the others with you in Galilee.

How would you feel? Afraid? Anxious? Guilt stricken? How will you act in anticipation of this meeting?

I'll bet guilt, the shame of betraying a friend and letting him down, fills your heart. This is how many of us feel when we let down a loved one.

Stories of the Lord's Resurrection and appearances leave us with a lot to ponder. We can't glean enough from the lessons.

For instance, isn't it fascinating that the first witnesses of the Resurrection are the last people to leave the foot of the cross after the Crucifixion? They are the three Marys who follow Jesus and hurry to anoint his body right after the Passover, on the third day. They are bold.

From their example, I learn that the Lord visits those who love him to the end despite the thorns and thistles they face. The risen Lord visits those hearts journeying through the route of pain and the cross. Scripture says, "If we died with the Lord, we shall live with the Lord" (2 Timothy 2:11).

There is something to say regarding the guilt-stricken and doubting disciples, too. For them, guilt and shame perhaps overwhelm the excitement that should have ushered in the Resurrection news. Many of Jesus' disciples let him down, or at least so it seems in their eyes. Ironically, Jesus is about to lift them—gradually, not in a shocking way, so their weak natures will mature in the understanding of the mercy of God.

Observe that Jesus takes many initiatives to disabuse their minds and restore their confidence. Recall that one of the beauties of the Christian faith is that it is God who searches for us. In Jesus' own words, "You did not choose me. I chose you and appointed you to go and bear fruit, fruits that will endure" (John 15:16).

Hence, Jesus first appears to the bold, the women, and then to the guilt-stricken Peter, the head of the apostles and the eleven. I might be wrong, but I feel there must be a reason why the bold women are the first to see the risen Lord.

Do you feel like the bold women, or do you feel like the disciples who let Jesus down? If it's the latter, are you afraid the truth will finally be known? Does guilt torment you? Is it difficult to hold your shoulders high and your face up, to look at the holy face of the risen Lord because of sin or guilt?

Allow your guilt and consequent doubt to be confronted by the risen Lord. Then you will see that although you let him down, he will lift you up to healing and grace.

REFLECT

I recall moments I have let the Lord down. What can I do differently now? How can I grow in my faith and respond boldly in a way that shows I treasure the values I say I cherish?

PRAY

I pray for the grace of a courageous makeover—conversion. Amen.

Alternative Reflection

Bold Witnessing

Readings: Acts 4:13–21; Mark 16:9–15

I re-emphasize the connection between a personal encounter with the Lord and passionate, bold witnessing. I will use Saint Peter's testimony when he and John are brought before the court as an example.

Previously, I mentioned that we have to witness the Lord and be a bold witness to others of what we've seen. This evangelization principle is essential to the quality and audacity of the witness.

In our relationships, we realize that familiarity with people increases the boldness of our testimony about them.

These days, I write quite a few reference letters for friends or former students seeking employment or admission to graduate school. Some reference letters take me fewer than twenty minutes to write. Others take up to two hours. I realize that the better I know candidates, the more freely and boldly I can write about their talents and skills. The less I know about them, the less confident I am about my reference for them.

This kind of thing happens in our spiritual lives as well. You notice that it is when the faith we profess becomes our own personal profession that we are passionate about it. In our lives as believers, the "we believe" has to be genuine. It has to turn to "I believe" for it to be authentic and audacious.

The Resurrection of the Lord Jesus Christ is striking to the apostles, the first witnesses of our faith. They have a personal connection with the Lord's mighty deeds. They know the Lord is risen. It isn't a delusion.

One of the impacts of the Resurrection is awareness of our spiritual blessings in Christ. This awareness inspires in us a new kind of courage. It is deeply personal, though it binds us together with the community of faith. It is the courage that is rooted in the fact that we have seen and heard. Thus, we believe. Saint Paul tells us that faith comes by hearing (Romans 10:17). The "hearing" is also the seeing. It is equally experiencing the workings of God in our lives and the lives of others. It is the witnessing of the saving grace of God in Christ.

Such a witness helps believers have a personal connection with the resurrected Lord. This personal connection increases our level of boldness in bearing witness to the saving grace of God. Our faith knowledge becomes bold as well. We speak because we love it. We speak because our experience is deeply personal, even though the community of faith shares it.

Peter and John are brought before the learned and experienced men in the Jerusalem temple to defend themselves and explain why they preach in the name of Jesus. They testify that he died and resurrected. The people notice their incredible boldness. Scripture reports, "Now when they saw the boldness of Peter and John and perceived that they were uneducated, common men, they wondered, and they recognized that they had been with Jesus" (Acts 4:13).

Peter and John don't just know *about* the Lord and his Resurrection. They *know* the Lord and his Resurrection. I ask you today: do *you* know the Lord, or do you simply know *about* the Lord?

REFLECT

To what extent am I aware of the values and blessings flowing from my faith? Am I aware of my gifts and talents and all the blessings I possess as a believer? How may I know and embrace them?

PRAY

Gracious God, give me the grace of deeper knowledge of Christ and the power of his Resurrection. Make me more aware of my gifts and blessings so that I can be a bold witness of your cause. Amen.

WEEK TWO OF EASTER

Divine Mercy Sunday

Immersed in Mercy

Readings, Year A: Acts 2:42–47; 1 Peter 1:3–9

Readings, Year B: Acts 4:32–35; 1 John 5:1–6

Readings, Year C: Acts 5:12–16;
Revelation 1:9–11A; 12–13; 17–19

Gospels, Years A, B, and C: John 20:19–31

*A*s I look at the picture of Divine Mercy (I suggest you fix your gaze on it too), I see mercy. I am reminded of the very nature of human weakness, the ugliness of sin, and the triumph of God's mercy.

Let me say this bluntly: sin is boring.

Do you know what's exciting? A sorrowful heart. It is when a repentant person comes before the one sinned against and is deeply sorry. Ask a priest at the confessional, and he will tell you. Ask parents with a problem child, and they will inform you. The joy of reconciliation surpasses many other human excitements.

Divine Mercy Sunday is a special day to be immersed in this most exciting aspect of the human relationship with God. Don't you realize that when God stares at the sinner, he looks with compassion? Don't you realize that when he gazes at a repentant sinner, he looks with mercy?

God's mercy isn't like ours. For us, mercy goes with memory. Many of us can forgive, but we can't forget. In our way of thinking, people must merit mercy. We have to make them pay for what they've done. Isn't this an integral part of our justice system? For us, mercy keeps records.

Divine Mercy is entirely different. No one merits it. No one can afford it. It is grace at its best. God forgives and deletes the memory of the sin, to use an imperfect human analogy. There is no longer any track record. God's mercy isn't dependent on restitution. Reparation can't, in a strict sense, remedy the infinite consequences of sin. God's priority isn't retribution either. It is reconciliation.

Divine Mercy is dependent on the merits of Christ's sorrowful Passion. God looks at the blood of his Son and looks down to see us at the foot of that cross, and his gaze is one of mercy and compassion. We'd better be at the foot of that cross where there is a generous outpouring of the blood and water of mercy.

It appears that, in terms of sin and the penitent repentant person, God does not look at the sinner and sin first. God looks first at the Son and through the Son to the sinner. In other words, God gazes on repentant sinners through the lens of his Son. The sinner becomes part of the Body of Christ. Thus, when God looks at that sinner, he sees the Redeemer's scars, wounds, and blood cleansing the wounds of the sinner's sin. God sees the Crucified in the sinner and showers mercy and healing. God touches the hearts and wounds of sinners with the healing balm of compassion.

It seems to me that the Divine Mercy Devotion signature—"Jesus, I trust in you"—is a constant appeal to this merit of the son for us. It's an example of immersion in Divine Mercy.

As we celebrate this special day of mercy, may we approach Jesus with humble acknowledgment of our need for mercy. May we come with contrite hearts and witness the excitement of reconciliation with God at Confession, the Great Sacrament of Mercy. May we also show mercy to others. Not because they merit it but because it is God's will for us having ourselves received mercy from God. And may our merciful hearts equally manifest themselves in corporal works of mercy for the unloved, the poor, the lonely, the imprisoned, the homeless, and addicts. May we bless everyone around us and our community with what Pope Francis called the "creativity of love."[1]

REFLECT
When gazing at the image of Jesus, represented in the Divine Mercy photo, what does it say to me about mercy and grace?

PRAY
O God, for the sake of your sorrowful Passion, have mercy on us and the whole world. Amen. Lord Jesus, make me your instrument and disciple of mercy and reconciliation to the wounded. Amen.

---

1. Pope Francis, Video Message to mark Holy Week, April 3, 2020.

Alternative Reflection

Beneficiaries of Divine Mercy

Readings, Year A: Acts 2:42–47; 1 Peter 1:3–9

Readings, Year B: Acts 4:32–35; 1 John 5:1–6

Readings, Year C: Acts 5:12–16;
Revelation 1:9–11A; 12–13; 17–19

Gospels, Years A, B, and C: John 20:19–31

*O*n this Divine Mercy Sunday, I reflect on God's mercy and how we are blessed to be its unmerited beneficiaries.

I am full of joy whenever I come out of the confessional, having confessed my sins to the Lord. I realize I don't necessarily deserve what I receive at God's throne of mercy. The healing, the joy, and the blessing of the divine life aren't necessarily due to the input of my own hands. It is God who gifts me with his life.

Right from the start of my faith life, I see God making the first move, all the time. As believers, we are people granted the grace of faith. We are called in love to communion with our Creator. It isn't because we merit it or because we are perfect. Fundamental Christian theology teaches us that God, our Creator, chooses us first. "You did not choose me. I chose you," says the Lord (John 15:16).

Another way to express this incredible grace is to say that God brings us to himself despite our weaknesses. God looks at us with mercy and kindness. God's love expressed in tender compassion gives us access to belongingness unto his life.

In mercy, we are begotten. In compassionate love, we are embraced. The Holy Father Pope Francis is spot on in describing God's merciful love for us as titled in his book: *The Name of God Is Mercy* (2016). Because of God's mercy, you and I have a shot at renewed life.

We read from one of the earliest Old Testament texts, Deuteronomy, how God's covenant with his people contains an essential attribute of mercy (see Deuteronomy 9:4–5). When God looks at us in our messiness, I doubt it is with the eye of justice. I believe it is with the sight of mercy, for no one can stand the justice of God.

Pope Saint John Paul II wrote about the fantastic reconciliation between God and us in *Dives in Misericordia*. He pointed to the truth that the mercy of God already invites us to restoration amidst our sins. God is abundantly rich in mercy. Here is an excerpt from the beautiful words of the pope: "Conversion to God always consists *in discovering his mercy*, that is, in discovering that love which is patient and kind (cf. 1 Corinthians 13:4) as only the Creator and Father can be . . . Conversion to God is always the fruit of the 'rediscovery' of this Father, who is rich in mercy."[2]

When I read the story of the covenant between God and Noah (see Genesis 9:8–15), I cannot but see that beyond the destruction of the flood is the mercy of God who restores. God also offers a sign of the rainbow as a symbolic reminder to generations that he forgives, shows mercy, and restores.

It isn't surprising to me that the first thing, the first Sacrament, the risen Lord speaks of to his disciples after the Resurrection is the sacrament of reconciliation. He tells them to go about being disciples of his reconciliation and mercy.

Scripture tells us the Lord institutes this sacrament on the evening of the first day of the week when he speaks to the timid disciples: "Peace be with you. As the Father has sent me, even so, I send you." And when he has said this, he breathes on them and says, "Receive the Holy Spirit.

---

2.   John Paul II, *Dives in Misericordia* (Vatican, 30 November 1980), no. 13.

If you forgive the sins of any, they are forgiven; if you retain the sins of any, they are retained" (John 20:19–23).

It is vital to the Lord that his people are healed and forgiven. He wants his people to receive the mercy he has established on the cross and the graces he pours from the Resurrection. He gifts the Church through this sacrament with the grace to be missionaries of this mercy.

We receive this grace in abundance when we go to confession, the sacrament of reconciliation. There we hear those words that bring us in touch with our Lord and restore us to spiritual health. Our sins are forgiven when we hear, "I absolve you from your sins in the name of the Father, the Son, and the Holy Spirit."

REFLECT
When was the last time I availed myself of the opportunity of going to confession? Do I realize that God's mercy awaits me no matter what?

PRAY
Thank you, Lord, for the grace of your mercy and healing. Thank you for everlasting compassion. Amen.

Monday

A Positive and Hope-Filled Attitude

Reading: Acts 4:23–31; John 3:1–8

*I*t fascinates me to see the sudden transformation that takes place in the lives of the early disciples after the Resurrection and Pentecost. We read how Peter and John return to the disciples and share their experiences (Acts 4:23–31). They do not do so timidly, as Peter was known for earlier in his life. Rather, they are passionate and courageous. The Lord transforms them from within.

We read how the Church unites in prayer and lifts their concerns to the Lord. We notice how, in their prayer, they reaffirm the great work of God. Amidst the trials, they aren't distracted from the great testimony of the miracles flowing from Christ.

They pray: "And now, Lord, look upon their threats and grant to thy servants to speak thy word with all boldness, while thou stretchest out thy hand to heal, and signs and wonders are performed through the name of thy holy servant Jesus" (Acts 4:29–30).

Subsequently, the Holy Spirit comes upon them. The Spirit strengthens them even more (verse 31) to boldly lead and share their testimonies.

I love this.

There is something to learn from this example of the early Church. The disciples have one key strategy when they are persecuted: they take their concerns, united in faith as believers in the Church, back to the Lord. They also refer to the great work of God. Such, I suggest, keeps them positive and less focused on current challenges that might have been discouraging for the young community.

A positive attitude is important in the testimony we share as children of the Resurrection. A hope-filled disposition is necessary for our spiritual comportment. No one who receives mercy and grace from the Lord goes home sad and depressed. No one who receives salvation fails to rejoice. No one to whom the risen Lord reveals himself remains unenthused by the power of the Lord. This positive attitude equips us to continue to share the joy and the Good News.

REFLECT

It doesn't take long before our faith's excitement meets the crunching experiences of human trials and tribulations. How do I respond when those sorts of experiences come my way? Do I bond with my fellow believers and unite in prayer or do I go it all alone?

PRAY

Lord, give me the grace of a positive and hope-filled attitude and the disposition to unite with my fellow believers and testify to your great works amidst current trials. Amen.

Tuesday

The Favor of the Apostles' Resurrection Witness

Readings: Acts 4:32–37; John 3:7b–15

*A*cts of the Apostles summarizes the activities of the first disciples and witnesses of the life of Jesus Christ. The book summarizes in a deliberate way the accounts of the life of the early Church as observed by a non-Jew medical professional, Luke.

Many believe that those actions or witnesses of the apostles could appropriately be called the acts of the Spirit of Jesus. One could also describe them as the acts of the Holy Spirit in the lives of the apostles. But only two of the apostles' activities are prominently documented, namely, Saint Peter's and Saint Paul's. Saints John's and James' stories are treated sparingly in the book.

The stories in Acts of the Apostles are compelling. Anyone who wants to learn how the early Church bears witness to the faith after the ascension of the Lord should first review Acts of the Apostles.

Today, I am particularly interested in Acts 4:33. It says, "With great power, the apostles bore witness to the resurrection of the Lord Jesus, and great favor was accorded them all."

The turning point in the apostle's faith journey is the fact of the Resurrection. From the news of the Resurrection, a new faith life begins for them. When the Pentecost comes, their preaching is invigorated by the clear message that Jesus is alive. He resurrected and is, therefore, the Lord.

Upon the Resurrection rests the decisive moment of the audacity of faith of the early disciples. Paul's conversion draws him to the daring truth of the Resurrection as well: "That I may know him and the power of his resurrection" (Philippians 3:10).

As believers, we do not need to be apologetic about the fact that Jesus resurrected. Upon this truth lies the boldness of our faith, at least in part. Without Easter, our faith as Christians would be empty.

In 2016, I had a one-on-one chat with Jim Caviezel, who portrayed Jesus in the 2004 film *The Passion of the Christ*. He alleged to having personal encounters with Christ during the filming that left a lasting impression in his heart. His experiences were so compelling that he talks about them regularly. He saw with his eyes and felt deep within his heart a glimpse of the Passion's truth. He claimed the impression has not left him since.

The Lord's Resurrection experience is so strong in the minds and hearts of the disciples of Jesus that it is a constant refrain on their lips. The confession brings additional favor too. Hear how Scripture describes it: "Great favor was accorded them all" (Acts 4: 33b).

Favor can also be translated as grace or blessing. The Christian blessing, favor, or grace flows from faith in the risen Lord. Constant recourse to the Christ of the Resurrection increases our spiritual wealth. Thus, we grow from grace to grace, favor to favor, glory to glory.

REFLECT
How strong is my faith in the Resurrection? In what ways may I allow it to shape my daily life?

PRAY
Lord, may my life and faith be firm in the truth of the Resurrection. May I and others receive divine favors through Christ, our Lord. Amen.

Wednesday

Resurrection—Luster of Life's Crown

Readings: Acts 5:17–26; John 3:16–21

*I*n the preceding reflection, I explained that the Resurrection brought renewed hope, favor, and enthusiasm to the apostles and disciples of Jesus. It is the same for us.

To be sure, in the history of salvation in Christ, the early disciples hold a unique place. Yet the graces of the risen Lord do not end with the early Church. Those graces continue to flow from generation to generation for anyone born anew in Christ.

Divine favors flow from the risen Lord. It is a blessing for us to hold on to this belief. Nevertheless, being witnesses of the Resurrection isn't always a bed of roses. It's a blessing with two sides—the rose and the temporal thorn.

Recall that right after the Resurrection's joys, Acts of the Apostles consistently shows the contrast of ridicule and the persecutions that follow. It's as if every victorious chant is cut short by boos. On and on, the circle continues, but in the end, glorious songs carry the day.

If you want a faith journey that doesn't come with persecutions, then Christianity isn't it. Right from the apostles' time until now, persecutions have been part and parcel of our Christian witness.

Acts of the Apostles 5:12–26, for instance, records the second prominent persecution against the apostles ordered by the high priest. The guards put the apostles in public jails. They endure a lot of torments. Many of the early disciples must have passed through profound psychological trauma too.

I recognize that many people detest persecutions. I do too. It's understandable and human. But if we are to hold on to the Lord's Resurrection's truth, we must expect ridicule and sometimes rejection.

We have to be prepared for the worst, though we are not to allow the worst things that happen to define us. Our courage as believers is to be proactive. We do not want persecutions or temptations to catch us off guard when they occur. Ultimately, we are to be vigilant, as Scripture suggests (1 Peter 5:8).

Get this straight: Christ has not promised us a faith life with only nice things; he certainly has not promised frosting on the cake. Instead, he has given us a living hope, joy, and boldness won on a crimson cross. This means, I suggest, that we win by fighting all the way through.

Glory lies in believing and witnessing to the risen Christ against all odds. Glory isn't won merely by believing the comfortable. It's won by swimming against the current.

G. K. Chesterton was spot on when he argued that "only live fish can swim against the current." Against the current is the luster of life's crown.

REFLECT

I hear the Lord tell me I am the light of the world and the salt of the Earth. It is a huge responsibility to lighten up the darkness and add a pleasant taste to life. In what ways may I be this light and this salt to my community and to those I meet?

PRAY

Lord Jesus Christ, give me the grace to swim against the current of darkness and be light and salt to whomever I meet and wherever I am. Amen. Fill me with joy as I do so. Amen.

Thursday

"We Must Obey God Rather Than Men"

Readings: Acts 5:27–33; John 3:31–36

A prominent pop artist whose name I prefer not to mention told me of the ordeals he experienced when recording music with the name of Jesus in the lyrics. Some in the entertainment industry warned him that this might cost him his career. He went ahead and produced the song as he was inspired to do. The music was a great success.

Nonetheless, some days later, he found he had lost many of those who networked for him in the circus of the power brokers in the music industry. In the long run, he lost a lot of money and connections.

"Though I have lost many of my friends," he told me, "I have not lost my joy."

I thank God for this young man who had the strength to be himself and stand up for his beliefs, even when it cost him a fortune. I continue to pray for him and ask you to keep him in your prayers too. Pray, also, for numerous others like him in the entertainment industry.

His story is similar to many in our world today, where it seems to be a bold Christian is tantamount to ridicule. Hence, many prefer to keep their faith private. This sort of reality is a kind of discrimination that dilutes the value of a particular group of people. It is simply wrong.

Do not allow anyone to make you think less of yourself or the values you cherish. It is self-defeating to censure yourself regarding the virtuous values or beliefs dear to your heart.

Are you shy about bearing witness to the Resurrected Lord? Are you afraid of persecution, of losing a friend or connections, of being sidelined, of losing money, or even of suffering emotional pain because of your faith? Courage! Learn from the boldness of Saint Peter and the apostles who reply to those who want to silence the gospel: "We must obey God rather than men" (Acts 5:29).

It could be that we are shy. Maybe we are unable to bear witness to the faith because we are inadequately informed about it. Maybe we do not believe it or love it enough. Maybe we have not developed a deep enough relationship with Christ to be confident about it and thus we are less passionate. If this is the case, we can do better.

I remember when I was going through the motions, even though I was already a baptized believer. I wasn't bold about my faith. By God's grace, all that changed when I encountered the Lord Jesus and the Holy Spirit in a deeply personal way. Praying the rosary and deepening my faith through a renewed life in the sacraments, especially the Eucharist and confession, and reading God's Word in Scripture were incredible channels of grace for me. They continue to nourish my spiritual life today.

In particular, daily visits to the Blessed Sacrament played a considerable role in my faith rediscovery. I began to see things differently. This changed everything for me.

Why not try this for yourself and see how your weakness can be transformed for God's glory? The risen Lord will grant you fresh enthusiasm for his cause.

REFLECT

Am I going through the motions in my faith journey? How may I hold the values of my faith life precious and be ready to celebrate it as who I am, not just something outside of me?

> **PRAY**
>
> God, inspire and enlighten the minds of my heart to love you and know you more. Restore to me the freshness of your love and my first love. May the memories of that first love experience keep me centered. Amen.

Friday

Daring Witness

Reading: Acts 5:34–42; John 6:1–15

*A*cts of the Apostles contains many examples of daring Christian witness by the early Church. Here is one: "When they [members of the council] had called in the apostles, they beat them and charged them not to speak in the name of Jesus, and let them go" (Acts 5:40).

The apostles' response is incredibly courageous and fascinating: "They left the presence of the council, rejoicing that they were counted worthy to suffer dishonor for the name (of Jesus). And every day in the temple and at home, they did not cease teaching and preaching Jesus as the Christ" (Acts 5:41–42).

Wow!

You might reply that this response was foolish. The apostles should have stopped when asked by the authorities to do so. They were daring legitimate authority, and this isn't right.

Were they irresponsibly daring? Isn't it equally true that the inability to stand up for one's legitimate rights harms a person's core identity?

I am reminded of the frequent occurrences in public spheres and during public discussions when people are discredited for holding particular religious views. Some choose not to express themselves and say they feel hushed to silence. The theory of the "spiral of silence," in which the mainstream silences alternate voices, is alive and well. This silencing mechanism is troubling for all people of goodwill. Isn't it a direct attack on freedom of speech that should be respected for all, no matter their religious or non-religious affiliations? Don't we live in a civil society where human rights are protected?

Though the apostles lived in a different time, they are examples of daring to speak what they believe. I pray never to put myself in a situation where I gag myself or am silenced by others. May I never, out of fear of being silenced, fail to be who I am. May God not let this happen to you either.

One of the terrible things that can happen to human freedom is to silence ourselves out of fear. Sometimes we silence ourselves because we make unethical compromises and deliberately choose what we know is evil simply because it's convenient. This harms our identity too.

May we be bold about our identity as believers in the risen Lord. May our words, gestures, and smiles resound with the echoes of Resurrection testimonials.

May our lives as believers always reflect our hope in the risen Lord. Amen. Resurrection is hope and joy to the world. Believers in the Resurrection bring much hope and joy to society. They're the light of the world and the salt of the earth. Boldness in living out our beliefs brings blessings to many.

Be bold. Shine the light!

REFLECT

Do I hold back from being who I am because of what people might say or because my values aren't popular? How can I remain authentic and celebrate the values of my faith?

PRAY

O Lord, give me the grace of gracious love and the courage to be open to others while cherishing and celebrating the values of the gospel that I love. Amen.

Saturday

Division of Labor

Readings: Acts 6:17; John 6:16–21

We continue to draw lessons from the early Church. I am thrilled by the apostles' leadership skills and level of discernment in resolving the issue of commitment to the practical works of mercy (see Acts 6:17).

Of course, the community is small. Perhaps this makes it easier to get organized. But those who run organizations know that human resource management isn't easy no matter how small the organization. Once you have more than one person to manage, you have to demonstrate effective leadership and managerial skills to be successful.

Concerning the early Church, we see that the Spirit leads the apostles to know their crucial mission. This enables them to know how to assign roles and share power in a way that promotes the gospel.

The Twelve Apostles are confident it would be wrong, a misdirected commitment, to leave the primary task of preaching the Word of God to serve at tables (Acts 6:2). Such would be a misplaced priority.

Thus, they select seven men, deacons, to serve at tables. Even in this selection, they have certain criteria. The people they choose must be those who are led by the Spirit. In other words, they must share the spirit of the gospel and be passionate about it. Note that the service of the table isn't completely disconnected from the service of the gospel; it's just that others may do this task better than some or are called with a primary mission to serve at the table or in other areas of life.

At least two key things are evident in this excellent leadership example within the early Church. First, the apostles know firsthand the very mission to which they are called and commissioned to lead the Church. They are focused on that primary mission. They aren't to put anything else, no matter how important, before this mission.

This is a huge lesson for ordained ministers, especially bishops and priests. Our primary call isn't to be managers of money. Though we oversee the church organization, our primary responsibility is to preach the Good News. We are ordained to bear witness to Christ through the Word and the Sacrament. If we are good at managing money but not the primary call of evangelization, we fail at our fundamental duty.

Second, the Twelve Apostles know how to work as a team. Theirs is leadership in collaboration rather than isolation. They listen to God's discerning grace to find the right kind of talents and passion. Their criterion for "Spirit-filled" personnel is a great model for selecting personnel for ministry.

God sure knows how to lead his people the right way. Focus on the mission. Other things will begin to align. Never be distracted because of social concerns, but do not ignore those concerns either. It is from the core mission that we become better agents of social change. The Christian model is animated. When we are animated by the Spirit of the Lord, our commitments to social affairs bear much fruit.

REFLECT

As a Christian leader, what is my primary mission in life? How am I allowing the Spirit to animate me in fulfilling the mission? In what ways do I balance prayer and service to the poor?

PRAY

Lord, grant me a centered life to focus on the essential things in my life and, from here, collaborate with others for effective social change. Amen.

WEEK THREE OF EASTER

Sunday, Year A

Encountering Christ

Reading: Acts 2:14, 22–33; 1 Peter 1:17–21; Luke 24:13–35

Visualize the two on the way to Emmaus (Luke 24:13–35), Cleopas and the other disciple whose name the Bible does not mention. The Lord Jesus, unrecognized, joins the conversation.

The Lord Jesus has given explicit instructions to the disciples to go to Galilee. He tells them they will see him there (Matthew 28:7; Mark 16:7). The women have reported the good news to the disciples early on Easter morning, and the Bible is clear: the two main places Jesus meets with some or many of the disciples is in Jerusalem (probably in the first days) and then in Galilee, as instructed.

The two disciples on the way to Emmaus choose to go in the opposite direction, away from Jerusalem. If we are to use Josephus' opinion of Emmaus's exact location as evidence, it means the two men head at least six to seven miles west. Thus, undoubtedly, they aren't going in the direction of Galilee either. Neither are they staying in Jerusalem where the rest of the disciples are. They are outrightly disregarding the Lord's instructions, which suggests they hardly believe in the Resurrection.

As they leave, their conversation reveals the hidden depressing thoughts locked in their minds. They seem to be utterly disappointed by Jesus' death. The tone of their conversation reveals their state of mind. They talk about Jesus using his human, biological name alone— Jesus of Nazareth—without reference to his identity as Christ. They also describe him as "a prophet mighty in deed and word . . ." (Luke 24:19), but Jesus isn't merely a prophet.

In their words, "We had hoped he [Jesus] was the one to redeem Israel" (24:21). Observe the tense they use, which denotes an obvious objection to who they think Jesus is. They equally express tacit disbelief regarding the news from the women concerning the Resurrection.

In this story, we see a summary of the doubts many people have about Jesus' identity. The two have similar doubts. Hence their frustration at his death.

Jesus, "the silent listener to every conversation," joins them in the conversation, but they don't recognize him. I wonder why they don't notice Jesus in their midst.

Many times, worries burden our hearts and even consume us. The result is that we can hardly see Jesus or hear his word. Our doubts are so loud that they deafen the ears of faith. Our disappointments are so deep that they blur our spiritual perception. Our problems seem so overwhelming that they sometimes prevent us from seeing that the Lord is here, walking with us, accompanying us. We are like the two on the way to Emmaus.

For instance, sometimes during the Eucharistic celebration, we do not focus because our anxieties consume us. Hardly do we remember the Lord beckoning us from the Eucharist, saying the words of his apostle, Peter, to us: "Cast all your anxieties on me, for I care about you (1 Peter 5;7). Hardly do we hear his own words: "Come to me, all who labor and are heavily laden, and I will give you rest" (Matthew 11:28).

From the encounter between these two and Jesus, we learn at least two things. First, good knowledge of Scripture opens our eyes to see the promises of the Lord, the prophecies. Walking by Divine Revelation is walking into a real understanding of our struggles and concerns. Hence, Jesus starts to unravel the riches of the Law and the prophets to these two. He shows how they point to him as the risen Lord, our hope and our joy.

Second, clarity about Divine Revelation is unpacked at the breaking of the bread. I understand some object to the meaning of the breaking of the bread as presented in Luke 24:30–31. Saint Augustine's interpretation that it is about the Eucharist has come to be accepted by many biblical scholars as correct. I uphold that too. The mysteries of divine conversation are constantly unwrapped at the breaking of bread, the Eucharist. In this sacrament, we see with better clarity what has set our hearts on fire as we hear the Word in Scripture.

We recognize the Lord is here. Our hope, and the answer to our queries, is in our midst and within us. In and with him, the pains of disappointment are, after all, short lived.

REFLECT

Sometimes I chose to do things my way. In my heart, I feel God is asking me to go in a different direction, but I know this course isn't what I want to do. I feel so vested in my way that it is difficult to leave it and change. How may I choose the right course, count my losses, and make a brave decision to follow the Lord's promptings?

PRAY

God, may I continue to encounter the risen Lord in the Word and the Eucharist, to open my eyes to recognize he is with me and is the way, the truth and the life. Amen.

Sunday, Year B

Christ in Our Midst

Readings: Act 3:13–15, 17–19; 1 John 2:1–5a; Luke 24:35–48

*O*n this third Sunday of Easter, I reflect on the fifth appearance of Jesus to his disciples after his Resurrection. The event is described in the Gospel of Luke 24:35–48. The Gospel of John 20:19–23 reports the same story with a few other details, such as when the Lord gives the apostles the power to forgive sins.

Here is the setting: Cleopas and another person whose name is not given hurry back from Emmaus after Jesus appears to them and has a long conversation with them. They hear the disciples share the news that Jesus has appeared to many people, including Simon. They share their own story, relating how they recognized Jesus by the breaking of bread (a pointer to the Eucharist) (see Luke 24:35).

They are still sharing their joy when the Lord Jesus appears to all of them. Read how the Gospel of Luke describes the event: "As they were saying this, Jesus himself stood among them, and said to them, "Peace to You" (Luke 24:36).

This visit of the Lord is unique in many ways, with fascinating details such as how the Lord encourages the apostles not to doubt what they have seen. It is also fascinating that Jesus shows them his hands and feet that have been pierced and asks them to touch him.

This passage also narrates how the Lord proves he is alive and not a ghost and asks the disciples for physical food. They give him a piece of baked fish, and he eats it in their sight. The passage also gives details of how he finally opens their minds to understand the deeper biblical truth that he is alive indeed, that he is the fulfillment of the prophecies in the Old Testament, that he is the reparation for our sins and the sins of the world (see 1 John 2:2). In him and through him, many receive divine forgiveness. He also tells them they are to bear witness to all they have seen.

The Lord's visit and his message of peace must have been a source of inspiration. The Lord comes at the right time, and he joins in our conversation at the perfect time.

He is in our midst to confirm our faith and our testimony about him. He encourages us and frees us from fear and doubt.

The Lord may not appear in physical form anymore as he did to the first witnesses, though he can if he chooses to. He chooses to appear to us in everyday life through the ordinary events of life. I see Christ every day when I have the privilege of breaking the bread and celebrating the Eucharist. In the Eucharist, I see his face and welcome his presence. He speaks and smiles and cuddles me. Sometimes, I startle for joy. Many times, I'm speechless at the warmth of his love.

I hear him through the pages of Scripture. In it, he maps out for me the way and grace of fullness of life.

I see him when I go to confession. I hear his words through the mouth of his priest reminding me that my sins are forgiven. "Do not be afraid" and "Go in peace . . ."

I see him in the people I meet in the workplace, at home, on the streets, and at recreational centers. I hear his voice whisper to me what I should do when I see the sick, the poor, the despairing, the immigrant, the marginalized, those in prison, the suffering, and the depressed.

I hear him loud and clear when I enjoy my meal with friends and then, suddenly, feel the need to provide a good meal for someone who doesn't have the privileges I have.

I see Jesus in our midst every day. I hear his voice. I gaze on his face. My neighbor is a signpost of the face of Jesus closest to me.

On this third week of Easter, I pray we see the risen Lord in our midst in everyday life. May we celebrate each moment as a touch of his presence.

REFLECT
In what ways do I meet Jesus in your everyday life? Where do I find Christ? How does Christ speak to me personally?

PRAY
Open my eyes, Lord, to see you and listen to you speak to me in ordinary life events so that I can be an audacious witness of your love. Amen.

Sunday, Year C

Saint Peter and the Pope—What Kind of Peter Do We Want?

Readings: Acts 5:27–32,40b–41; Revelation 5:11–14; John 21:1–19 or 21:1–14

I draw a lesson from Saint Peter as the first pope (in Greek, the word is *pappas*, meaning father) of the Universal Church and some of its implications for the office of the pope.

People sometimes say—explicitly or implicitly—that the pope, the Holy Father, has to be perfect; otherwise, he relinquishes his authority as the leader of the Church. Those familiar with church history recognize this is an old debate.

What kind of Peter do we want? A perfect Peter, one who has all the impeccable perfection of the angels? Is this a Peter who never falters or waivers? Is this a Peter who isn't human and who thoroughly follows the ways of the Lord?

If this is the kind of Peter we want, then we don't want the biblical Peter.

The biblical Peter is born like we are, in sin. The Lord chooses him from his humble profession as a fisherman to lead his holy body, the Church (see Matthew 4:18–20). The biblical Peter makes humbling mistakes and commits venial and grave sins. You may read the following verses as proof: Matthew 16:21–24, John 18:10–11, and Matthew 26:69–75; see also Luke 22:54–62, John 21:1–22, and Galatians 2:9–14.

The biblical Peter isn't a bundle of academic excellence either. Some would argue he's not much of a thorough thinker. He is unstable in many ways and afraid in many others.

We notice he is a rustic fisherman, not always properly dressed (John 21:7).

We read about his unguarded and audacious zeal (Matthew 26:35; John 18:10–11; Matthew 14:28), yet see his unmistakable fears, doubt, and weak faith (Matthew 14:30–31; John 18:15–18, 25). He is enthusiastic, but he rarely follows through with his commitments.

He is the one who goes back to fishing and perhaps inspires the other six disciples to join him in their old profession (John 21:3) even though the Lord asks them to wait in Galilea. They are to become fishers of men, not fishermen. He is presented as one who is impatient.

Yet it is this same Peter who takes the lead. He wants to serve. He tells the disciples to venture out. He hauls the net when the Lord asks him to do so. He pioneers many of the actions that lead to the growth of the early Church.

No, he isn't perfect, yet his zeal and love for the Lord are evident all the way. Somewhat aware of his imperfections, he constantly repents when he falters. In him, the precious grace of ongoing conversion is real and live. He is quick to recognize his sins, as when he says, "Depart from me, Lord. I am a sinful man" (Luke 5:8). He is the right candidate for heavenly renewal. This is the Peter the Lord calls and tells three times to feed and tend his sheep, the Church (John 21:17–19).

If anyone is in doubt as to the Lord's ways in the leadership of the Church, let them read the Bible. If anyone doubts the necessity of central authority in the Church, let them read John 21:17–19.

The pope isn't a man of his own. He is a man chosen and called to lead the Body of Christ. The pope isn't expected to be perfect. The Lord himself never uses perfection as a criterion. Neither should we as believers. No one is perfect except the Lord. The Holy Father is holy because the Body of Christ, of which he is the physical head, is holy.

This doesn't mean the pope isn't called to holiness of life. He is. To whom much is given, much is expected, the Lord tells us (Luke 12:48). To whom much is given, to that person, the devil's attacks are prime. The pope needs our ceaseless prayers.

Here is the most incredible aspect of this grace of the papal office: the Lord himself sustains it. "The Gates of the netherworld cannot overcome it" (Matthew 16:18).

You can choose to believe the Lord is God and hang on to his Word and the ways and means by which he leads his Church, or you can choose to explain it away and subvert it with empty philosophy. It is a blessing to hold on to God's word.

As for me, I follow the ways of the Lord. I listen, and I obey.

REFLECT
What can I do to support the Church as the Body of Christ? In what ways may I commit to offering prayers and sacrifices for the leaders of my church who are immediate targets of the evil one?

PRAY
Lord, I pray for the grace of the virtue of piety and obedience. Amen.

Monday

Learning from Saint Stephen

Readings: Act 6:8–15; John 6:22–29

*H*ow do you read the story of the models or saints of our faith? Do their stories resonate with yours? During today's reflection, I will share one of the ways I relate with the saints, those called the Church Triumphant in our Catholic tradition.

I read the saints' stories as my story. I see them as real human beings with many flaws who welcome the grace of transformation. I see in their lives mine in the making. I tap from them some of the ways to lead a holy life. Take, for instance, Saint Stephen, whose witness to the risen Lord is recorded in Acts of the Apostles, chapters six and seven.

Stephen is one of the seven deacons (the first deacons of the Church) appointed by Saint Peter to serve food in the early Church. In addition to serving food, Stephen serves God's Word. He sees the connection between both.

Consider what happens when someone invites you to dinner. In many cultures, dinners are the best times for sharing because people engage in stimulating discussions. Hence, dinners offer fellowship. I am not talking about forced meals, the kind where parents make their kids eat lots of vegetables. "Vegetables are good for you, child," my mom used to persuade. At the time, those were horrible tastes. Some of the foods we have to eat because we are on medications aren't enjoyable either, but I'm talking about sharing delicious meals with people you love. Such dinnertimes are refreshing.

You may have noticed the subtle connection between food and words. Food feeds the body. Words—including thoughts and ideas—feed the mind, the soul, and the spirit. One's mind, soul, and spirit are as good as the words and thoughts that settle in. There is one food that feeds body, mind, soul, and spirit—the Eucharist, the Bread of Life.

The seven deacons' call is to serve, not only at social gatherings but also, more importantly, at the breaking of bread, the Eucharist. Thus, immersed in the Eucharistic spirituality, Deacon Stephen shares the Word of God with others who are not members of the faith.

Eucharistic participation enables us to be at the service of God and his people through words and deeds. Also, the strength of the meal empowers us to bear witness to the risen Lord.

Hear how Scripture speaks of the testimony of Stephen: "Stephen filled with grace and power, was working great wonders and signs among the people" (Acts 6:8–15). His testimony about his faith in the risen Lord through the Holy Spirit's power cost him his life. However, as I will reflect tomorrow, he remains an incalculable asset of courageous faith.

In effect, I draw from the saints the courage to bear witness to the Gospel of Christ even when it entails martyrdom. The saints teach us many things. Among them is how to be men and women of the courage of faith in a world where anything goes.

REFLECT

Who is my favorite saint? What attracts me to that saint? What may I learn from him or her?

PRAY

Lord, you touched the saints' lives and inspired them to be courageous and loving witnesses to your resurrection power. Grant me the same grace to bear fruit that endures. Amen.

Tuesday

Look Up!

Readings: Acts 7:51–81a; John 6:30–35

We return to the story of Saint Stephen, the first Christian martyr. Acts of the Apostles provides a gripping account of Stephen's last words before he dies. Please read that story. It has many things to teach us about bold witnessing. Let me share a portion of it: "Stephen, filled with the Holy Spirit, looked up intently to heaven and saw the glory of God and Jesus standing at the right hand of God" (Acts 7:55).

Watch the pattern in this story. Stephen, *filled with the Holy Spirit, looked up.* Then he *saw the glory of God* and *Jesus standing* at his right hand.

Many times, we fail to see the risen Lord and Savior Jesus Christ because we look down. Our trials, tribulations, worries, or crosses suck us in, get in our heads, and pull us face down. Like the women who come to the tomb to anoint Jesus, looking for him in the grave, we tend to assume all hope is lost. We need divine words reassuring us as the angel reassured the women: "He is not here." I love this reassurance! Our hope isn't in the grave. He has risen. Look up!

But, more often than not, our worries get the better of us, consume us, and prevent us from looking up. We can't seem to put our worries behind us. Our gazes point downward instead of upward. As the Book of Psalms says, we fail to see that our help is in the name of the Lord, the Maker of heaven and Earth (see Psalms 124:8).

When we look up, either to heaven or up to Christ, we can see the glory of the risen Lord. We can be bold, like Stephen, to announce what we see. We are messengers of the Good News. When we look up, we see the hope and the future illumined with the bright light of grace.

Though this may cost us a lot, it will not take away the hope and joy that we share in the risen Lord. For instance, Stephen's martyrdom isn't the end of the story but the beginning of a new chapter of grace. Likewise, situations of trials aren't the end of the story. The saints' witness is the spice of the Earth, bringing life and hope to many who are bowed down and continually looking down.

If you want to have the courage of the apostles to bear witness to the Lord, look up! Your inspiration comes from God. God will inspire you to inspire his people.

Reflect

When troubles come my way and challenges occur, do I look down in despair or do I look up to God from whom saving grace comes? How can I avoid being drowned by the problems I face?

Pray

I pray for the grace to look up when burdened. It is by looking up to the Lord that my salvation comes. Amen.

Wednesday

Tap from History

Readings: Acts 8:1b–8; John 6:35–40

*H*istory has a lot to teach us. Knowledge of history can inspire and empower us for greater things.

Take, for instance, the history of the Church. Reading from Acts of the Apostles to the very recent history of the Church in our contemporary world reminds me that we have much to learn.

In reviewing Church history, I made some discoveries. One has to do with a pattern that I believe is significant.

The two thousand-plus years of the Church may be grouped into two non-chronological phases that follow a pattern. There are phases of considerable spiritual growth and evangelization when the Church suffers great persecutions from the outside world and does not dine with those who wield political powers. Examples abound from the early Church to the Roman persecutions, from Emperor Nero to Decius, Valerian, Diocletian, Galerius, and into the medieval period as well as the Renaissance.

Persecutions, trials, and sufferings bring out the best in the Church, proving what Jesus said: "If you want to be my follower, take up your cross and follow me" (Matthew 16:24).

In contrast, review the Church's history throughout the times she is buddies with those in political power or in those periods the Church wants to be like the world. She becomes so comfortable that she stops being the "salt of the earth" and "the light of the world" (Matthew 5:13–14).

A recent example is the grave evils of the sexual scandals running from the 1960s into the early '90s. The Church was so comfortable that some ministers lost sight of their calling. Comfort devoid of sacrifice is the seed of Church decay, and in the process, the weak become victims. Though the Lord Jesus has promised the gates of the netherworld will not overcome the Church, many souls can be lost because of scandals.

A persecuted Church is a thriving Church. This idea isn't merely mine. It is the wisdom of the Church. Recall the famous quotation of Tertullian, a second-century Church father from Africa: "The blood of martyrs is the seed of the Church."

A line in Acts 8 describes how persecution leads to the spreading of the gospel: "Now those who were scattered went about preaching the Word" (Acts 8:4). The persecution of the early Church endorsed by Saul led to the spread of the gospel to distant lands.

Many times, people ask how we can lead a more proactive approach to evangelization. Here is how: begin denying yourself, be ready to suffer, and go beyond your comfort zone, serving others and prepared to endure opposition. Doing so equips you and the Church for effective evangelization.

Remember, this doesn't mean forcing your opinion on others. That would be the opposite of true evangelization. It means professing and proposing the truths you hold dear. The world forces its will, not the Christian. Believers, though bold, are gentle, wise as an owl, and innocent as a dove.

REFLECT

What lessons do I learn from the Church's history, especially those times the Church passed through dark experiences? Does this history discourage me or does it renew my commitment to hold on to the faith? Do I embrace the Lord's promises that the gates of hell will not prevail?

> **PRAY**
> I pray that the true spirit of evangelization, not discouraged by suffering, will continue to inspire us. Amen.

Thursday

Follow the Lead

Readings: Acts 8:26–40; John 6:44–51

*P*reviously, in the reflection of Tuesday of the third week, I shared how evangelization thrives amidst persecution. Here, I continue with the same theme or, to use a more contemporary concept, with New Evangelization.

As you may know, New Evangelization in Christianity, for the most part, is about bearing witness to the life of Christ. It is witnessing to the Good News of Christ, the news of salvation to every part of society, wherever people are. It is also about being agents of renewal through the power of the Spirit to those cultures and peoples who used to believe but no longer have the same zeal they once had. You might say it is renewal and "in-servicing" with and in the life of Christ. For more systematic definitions, I suggest reading *Evangelii Nuntiandi of Pope Paul VI* and *Evangelii Gaudium (the Joy of the Gospel)* by Pope Francis.

Evangelization is the work of the Holy Spirit. The Holy Fathers call the Holy Spirit "the principal agent of evangelization."[3] The Holy Spirit has a way of directing us to where there are needs for renewal. The Spirit uses people, circumstances, events, and sometimes heavenly angels to lead us. If we listen, we can speak, evangelize, and bear witness to Christ's rejuvenating life.

Sometimes, God directs us through his angels. Scripture calls these angels "ministering spirits sent forth to serve, for those who are to obtain salvation" (Hebrews 1:14).

Some biblical instances show how God's angels can lead us to what the Lord wants and how we may start. A fantastic example involves the story of Philip, one of the seven deacons in Acts of the Apostles.

Scripture says this: "An angel of the Lord said to Philip, 'Rise and go toward the South to the road that goes down from Jerusalem to Gaza' . . . and he rose and went" (Acts 8:26–27).

Consequently, he follows the lead and evangelizes an influential Ethiopian. The latter needs a teacher to explain to him the prophecy he is reading.

Many times, we look for a lead from God. We are discerning what to do, where the Lord is leading us, and how we can do it. Sometimes it seems we can't find a lead.

I often find that those nearing retirement are concerned about "What's next?" All their years as younger people, they planned how to retire, but once they are in their middle fifties onward, a weird feeling of "What's next?" grips them.

We have the lead, only we may not be silent enough to listen. Let it not be that we are too busy to pay attention to the whispers of God telling us what to do.

---

3. Pope Paul VI, Apostolic Exhortation *Evangelii Nuntiandi* (Vatican City: December 8, 1975), no. 75. See also John Paul II, Encyclical Letter *Redemptoris Missio* (Vatican City: December 7, 1990), no. 21.

God sends his angels to minister to our needs, providing us with the lead we seek. Don't you realize that each of us has a guardian angel whose sole job is to guide us at God's command? "He has put his angels in charge of you, to guide you in your ways" (Psalms 91:11).

God's "angels" can also come in the form of advice from a friend, family member, or even a co-worker pointing out something we've never before taken seriously. They can come in the form of the intuition we need to change a particular line of action. They can come from an idea we have while listening to a boring sermon.

The angel is the helping hand we need when we need it most. It might be the unusual visitor who asks you out for dinner. It could be the pet in the house reminding you what loyalty and faithfulness are. It could be a dream you have to scale the heights of your aspirations.

Follow the lead. There is no need to procrastinate.

REFLECT
Many people have come into my life or crossed my path and become like angels. They have helped me in numerous ways to become who I am today. In what ways have I helped others? In what ways have I become the angel someone else has encountered?

PRAY
Thank you, Lord, for all the people you have inspired to help me. May I do the same for others. Amen.

Friday

Why Are You Persecuting Me?

Readings: Acts 9:1–20; John 6:52–59

*Y*ou are probably familiar with the following biblical question: "Why are you persecuting me?"

The Lord Jesus Christ appears in a vision to ask this question of Saul, who later becomes Paul, when Saul is headed to Damascus to arrest believers in the Lord and bring them back to Jerusalem to execute them.

Saul doesn't know whose voice he hears, so he asks who is speaking. The Lord Jesus replies, "I am Jesus, who you are persecuting" (see Acts 9:1–20).

Every time I read this story, just like many other events in the Bible, it has new meaning.

Saul is from Tarsus. He is a tentmaker as well as a smart attorney. He is also extremely enthusiastic about defending the Law of Moses. Because of his belief, temperament, and influence, he takes the lead to exterminate the early Church. He is ignorant of the implications of what he is doing. He thinks he is doing something good for God.

From this story, we know how Jesus feels when his body, the Church, is maligned and persecuted. We also understand the depth of the relationship of the believers—as the Body of Christ—with Christ. Believers are the Body of Christ. As such, they are in him and he is in them.

This truth is even more vivid at the Eucharist when we eat the body and drink the blood of Jesus. As the Lord Jesus says, "He who eats my bread and drinks my blood remains in me and I in him" (John 6:56).

Mother Angelica, the founder of the Eternal Word Television Network (EWTN), once shared a witty conversation she had with her friend, Dr. Alice von Hildebrand, who was Jewish before she converted to Catholicism. Mother Angelica joked that she herself is as Jewish as her friend because she receives Christ's body and blood every day in the Holy Eucharist. In other words, she said, "We are what we eat."

On another note, Saul's story makes me ponder how the Lord looks at us when we, members of his body, tear each other apart. It is sad to see how negative and polarizing so many believers are.

In days past, it was unbelievers who vehemently attacked the Church for obvious reasons. Today, on social media platforms, it is Church members who spew the most vitriol against the Body of Christ. Believers and faith-based organizations tear each other apart in cyberspace. Calling each other names, they use words no decent person would use against anyone. At the same time, unbelievers watch and feast on the spoils. Instead of being the light of the world, we all too often let worldly hate, resentment, bitterness, and hypercriticality become our torchbearer.

Even within the Church, we wash our dirty linens in public, claiming we are pointing out errors. Indeed, we should correct errors, not share digital texts, sounds, images, and videos across the web with people who do not share our faith tradition. Doing so isn't a sign of virtue. More to the point, it is a disgrace to the Body of Christ to draw traffic to our online media platforms by appealing to humanity's worst instincts. The Lord would speak from heaven, "Why are you persecuting me?"

I wonder what has become of the Christian virtue of piety. I wonder where the traditional virtues of charity have gone. Saint Paul tells us we can have the most outstanding charisms and speak with the most prophetic voices, but without true love, Christian charity, it is all empty (1 Corinthians 13:1–3).

Growing up reading the lives of the saints and falling in love with their exemplary Christian lives, one of the no-nos I learned to avoid was a censorious spirit. This spirit looks for faults and is quick to criticize. Such spirits persecute Christ instead of building the Church.

May we learn from the story of the conversion of Saul that we are Christ's body. May we help build this Church. United with Christ and the rest of the Body of Christ, may we help heal and bind the wounds of this body.

REFLECT

Do I see in the wounds of Church members a scandal to my faith? Or do I realize that Christ has not given us a perfect body but a church that bears the mark of the wounded Messiah? Do I help in the healing process? How do I contribute to healing this Body of Christ?

PRAY

Lord, make me an instrument of your healing grace wherever I find myself. Amen.

Saturday

Generosity Meets Generosity

Saturday: Acts 9:31–42; John 6:60–69

*T*he town of Joppa was a seaport area. Before the nineteenth century, it was the only place people could rest en route to Egypt and Mount Carmel. It was technically the seaport for Jerusalem, the main port of the coast whose name today is Jaffa. Bustling with life, music, and dynamism, Joppa was relatively wealthy. Tel Aviv was eventually founded on its outskirts.

Like many seaport towns, Joppa housed the very wealthy. It was also a home for the lower class on the economic ladder who took care of travelers' needs and helped them with small jobs. Prostitution rings were common, and the vulnerable were exploited.

In that city, a wealthy woman saw it as her bounden duty to improve the living standards of the poor women and widows. In ancient Israel, widows were counted with orphans and foreigners as the *anawims*—the poorest of the poor. They were among the most vulnerable of all. At that time, widows lost virtually every inheritance and protection at the death of their husbands, making them easy prey to manipulative users and abusers. At Joppa, there were no limits to the harm to which widows could be exposed.

Wherever there is a need, God provides by sending his angels and saints. Needs drive swift and divine intervention. Needs propel the best human creativity. Needs should be met. This is how God has made things, set them in *statu via* (in process), so that we can be part of bringing about his providence in our world. We are God's hands and feet for providence.

God meets needs through people like you and me, people who pay attention to what is going on around them. People with generous hearts meet needs.

God's angel, the wealthy woman in Joppa, was a very pretty woman who was determined to provide for the local women. Her Hebrew name, Tabitha, translated in Greek as Dorcas, means gazelle or deer. Deer and gazelles are beautiful creatures, aren't they?

Names have significant meanings in Hebrew culture just as they do in African cultures. People in these cultures do not give names arbitrarily. Every name has a meaning tied to the time, the culture, the lineage, or the events surrounding the child's birth.

The deer is need driven, and so are our hearts and souls for God. The Biblical imagery about the deer comes to mind—the soul thirsts like a deer thirsts for a fresh running stream (see Psalms 42:1).

Like Dorcas, the deer is considered lovely, gentle, and bright-eyed. Dorcas believes in the Lord Jesus. Her faith is exemplary in her work of generosity to the poor of Joppa, especially widows.

She is God's answer to the needs of widows at Joppa, and I hope we are God's answers to someone else's needs. It's a beautiful thing to do and be.

Dorcas' generosity isn't like ours. We donate to charity, a beautiful gesture, but we seldom want to get our hands and feet dirty with the actual service of delivering gifts, handing them out, and visiting with the poor in the slums. Many of us don't want to get involved with the sticky, dirty, messy stuff. It is easier to just give money.

Dorcas gives money and, above all, makes tunics herself to give away. What a labor of love! She gives clothes to the widows with her own hands and visits with them too. See how the Bible describes her: "She was completely occupied with good deeds and almsgiving" (Acts 9:36).

When Dorcas dies, the widows' cries reach God. They invite Peter to pray for Dorcas; they are expecting a miracle. In effect, they beckon the Apostle Peter to ask God to restore their hope. God does, and the miracle of raising the dead occurs.

Saint Peter speaks real life to the woman who has given hope to many, and she receives her life back. We hear from the Lord himself that "the words that I have spoken to you are spirit and life" (John 6:63).

Here is a thought: as we meet human needs, God meets our needs too and we receive life in abundance. We do not receive merely earthly life but healing grace, the life that endures. Be generous to those in need. Your generosity will win divine benevolence for you too, so get busy with a labor of love. Remember, the measure we give is the same that we shall receive in return, and even more. As Scripture says,

"Good measure, pressed down, shaken together, running over, will be put into your lap" (Luke 6:38).

If I may ask, when was the last time you were generous with your time, talent, or treasure? When was the last time you gave back to your community?

REFLECT

Do I have a regular program of using my time, talent, or treasure to serve others? How do I follow through with this commendable commitment?

PRAY

Lord, like Dorcas in the Bible, may my generosity to the poor be not just the gift of materials such as money, clothes, or food but also the gift of my time. May my generosity flow from deep love and respect for the beneficiaries as people who are my equal, not inferior or beggars. Amen.

WEEK FOUR OF EASTER

Sunday, Year A

Learning from Christ, the Good Shepherd

Readings: Acts 2:14a, 36–41; 1 Peter 2: 20b–25, John 10:1–10

Good Shepherd Sunday is celebrated on the third Sunday of Easter (in the Eastern Rite, and Latin Rite pre-Vatican II) or fourth Sunday of Easter (in the Latin Rite since Vatican II). This day is also called Vocation Sunday, emphasizing Christ's call to ministerial service in his body, the Church. Thus, it is a Sunday to reflect on the graces and Good News of Christ, the Good Shepherd. Hopefully, this reflection will help us in our various vocations, in particular the vocation to the ministerial priesthood.

Let us unite with the Universal Church in praying for vocations— vocations to the priesthood, to the diaconate order, and to religious life. Let us equally pray for vocations to holy matrimony. I believe that all four are connected. If we have stronger families, open to life and rooted in our Catholic Christian identity, we can inspire our children to the priestly and religious life. If we need younger vocations, we equally need Catholic families to be genuinely pro-Christ, entirely in support of life, the Church, and Holy Orders.

One may ask: must we pray for vocations? Is the role of the ordained minister necessary? I will respond by taking us back to the life of Christ as well as the role of Christ as the Good Shepherd. I use the Gospel of John, chapter ten, as a primary source.

Jesus Christ has performed an incredible miracle of healing a man born blind in John 9. Only God can do this. Some of the Jewish authorities try everything possible to explain away the miracle. When the man insists that Jesus must be of God and refuses to deny the miracle, the Jewish authorities expel him from the temple (John 9:34), which means he is barred from being part of the worshiping community. The door is shut against him.

As I explained in a previous reflection, within the Jewish community, being expelled from the temple is the most terrible possible rejection. It means the person is excluded from divine worship and salvation. If the expulsion is permanent, it means the person is condemned for life.

But is this man condemned for life? Not if the true Good Shepherd is his faith. While expelled, Jesus seeks him out. Know this: when you are dismissed, rejected, or the door shuts against you because you are doing good things or are a believer, the Good Shepherd searches for you. You are not alone. God is with you. Emmanuel (God with us)!

When Jesus finds the man, he starts the excellent teaching about his mission as the Good Shepherd. Though the door is shut to the man who has been healed from blindness, Jesus points to him, to the Jews listening, and indeed to us, saying that he himself is the door (the gate): "Truly, truly, I say to you, 'I am the door of the sheep'" (John 10:7). Jesus doesn't say he is a door *of* the sheep but *the* door, *the* gate. Thus he excludes the possibility of the sheep finding a true saving pasture via sources other than by him.

This is an incredible and audacious claim. It's a claim that the Church, following the teachings of the apostles, has given the general theme of "salvation is in Christ."

For the man born blind, it is a refreshing message. To know that the door shut against him isn't the door of his salvation is encouraging.

Jesus is the door for good reasons. First, to know him and believe in him, to walk in his footsteps, is salvation.

Second, he gives life to the sheep and not just biological or physical life; he gives divine life that lives forever. The French theologian Reginald Garrigou-Lagrange, considered one of the greatest moral theologians of the twentieth century, said that eternal life is the greatest of human aspirations and values. The Lord Jesus grants the sheep that eternal life, the divine life.

Hence, the desire of all hearts is found in Christ and is achieved through him. He is the gate. As he says, "I am the way." He is equally the Good Shepherd because he leads us to the truth: "I am the truth." He is the sheep as well: "I am the life." By laying down his life for his sheep through his death and resurrection, the greatest sacrifice of all time, Jesus Christ is not merely a teacher. He is the priest, the victim, and the sacrifice. He is the Lord.

At least four qualities of Christ as the Good Shepherd are evident here:

1. He searches for those shut out of access to salvation (see John 9:34–35) to bring them to greener pastures. Meditate on the message of Psalm 23: "The Lord is my shepherd." Even when the sheep stray, God keeps searching and reaching out for them. Remember the three parables of forgiveness in Luke 15, also called the Three Parables of Mercy? Hence, we must pray for shepherds (Church leaders), whose primary call and desire is to follow the Good Shepherd and search for people who have strayed from the route of salvation. Caring for souls is the primary call of the shepherd who follows the example of Christ, the Good Shepherd.

2. He lays down his life for his sheep. To be a good shepherd is to be able to sacrifice for the sheep. Jesus, the Good Shepherd, bears the weaknesses of the sheep and suffers so the sheep can live. So, turn, we pray for vocations and shepherds (Church leaders) who will be ready to be victims so that God's children will find hope and peace. Pray for the grace of heroic sacrifice and service.

3. As the Good Shepherd, Jesus leads the way: "He goes before them, and the sheep follow him . . ." (John 10:4). Jesus is a true servant leader who leads the way even when the route is rough and turbulent. We pray for shepherds who will be courageous to lead and serve as Christ did amidst the hazards connected with the priestly and religious life.

4. Finally, Jesus comes so that we will have an abundance of life. That is his mission as the Good Shepherd (see John 10:10). Though we can never give people "life to the fullest," we can be vehicles through which this sanctifying grace is granted to them. We pray for vocation to the priesthood so that no person, no matter where they live, is deprived of an opportunity to receive the sacraments and God's Word.

Hence, if eternal life starts here with the seed of eternal life in our souls, and if the seed of eternal life comes through sanctifying grace that reaches us through the sacrament and the Word, and if, without ordained ministers (especially priests), we can't have most of the sacraments, isn't it necessary to pray for vocations to the sacred priesthood?

As Saint Pope John Paul II said in his encyclical letter, *Ecclesia de Eucharistia,* "Without the priest, there will be no Eucharist." It follows then that without the priest, channels of sanctifying grace are highly limited. The need to pray for vocations to the priesthood is urgent.

Join me in asking the Good Shepherd to touch people's hearts to say "Yes" to God's promptings to become priests and deacons and to embrace a religious life.

REFLECT

In what ways do I promote the vocation to ordained ministry or religious life? In what ways do I foster an appreciation for the sacrament of matrimony? What can I do to help encourage vocations in my family and community? To the best of my knowledge, are there persons whom my life has inspired to consider my kind of vocation?

PRAY

Lord, I pray that those afraid of permanent union through the sacrament of holy matrimony will embrace it. May they also be open to full love and life, including procreation. Give me the grace to discover or celebrate my vocation in life. Amen.

Sunday, Year B

Seven Qualities of the Good Shepherd

Readings: Acts 4:8–12; I John 3:1–2; Jn 10:11–18

I share a pastoral application of the qualities of the Good Shepherd hinted at in the Gospel of John 10:1–18. I do so not as a scholarly piece but as a way to engage in spiritual contemplation of the role of Christ as the Good Shepherd.

Joe and Nancy had a terrible year. Their child had barely survived a drug overdose. His life had become a constant painful struggle for him and the entire family. Joe's mom had not been doing well either. From one case of depression to chronic panic attacks, the family had been through the darkest months of their lives.

Amid their struggles, the pastor of their church paid regular visits. Sometimes he prayed with them. Other times he brought them Holy Communion, anointing them with the Oil of the Sick. From time to time, he mentioned their intentions during Mass and often reassured them of his prayers. On several occasions, he said only one or two words and was simply present with them.

Months passed, and the crisis slowly faded. Joe and Nancy felt God was with them throughout it all. For them, the human instrument God used was their pastor. "He is indeed a good pastor," they said.

What does it mean to be a good pastor, and have you wondered why the leader of your parish is called a pastor?

"Pastor" comes from a Latin word that in English means shepherd. It is a title borrowed right from God's imagery as our shepherd and his people as his sheep (see Isaiah 40:11; Ezekiel 34:11–31). Our Lord

Jesus Christ uses the same imagery and personalizes it since he is the "Good Shepherd" (John 10:11).

Drawing from the prophecies of Isaiah, Ezekiel, and the Gospel of John 10, the Second Vatican Council's document on the Church beautifully captures this teaching: "The Church is a sheepfold whose one and indispensable door is Christ. It is a flock of which God Himself foretold He would be the shepherd, and whose sheep, although ruled by human shepherds, are, nevertheless, continuously led and nourished by Christ Himself, the Good Shepherd and the Prince of the shepherds, who gave His life for the sheep."[4]

We read from the Gospel of John how Jesus Christ teaches this truth about himself: "I am the Good Shepherd" (John 10:11). He goes ahead to tell us some of the qualities of the Good Shepherd:

1. The Good Shepherd willingly lays down his life for the sheep (John 10:11, 15, 17). He makes the greatest sacrifice of all: he offers his life for the sheep. For a pastor to be a good shepherd is to share in this commitment by willingly undertaking daily sacrifices for the welfare of those we serve.

2. The Good Shepherd does not carry out the shepherding role for pay (John 10:12). Nothing is found in the life and ministry of Jesus of Nazareth, the Christ, that is pay-for-service. If a pay-for-service model inhabits the work of pastoring, one wonders if it is consistent with the role of the Good Shepherd.

3. The Good Shepherd is passionately committed to the sheep's care but not as a hired shepherd (John 10:13). The passion to care for the sheep is primary. It is not a result of what financial benefits will come from it but simply because the shepherd wants the sheep to find assistance and green pastures. Pastoral life is first and foremost a commitment to the

---

4. Second Vatican Council, Dogmatic Constitution on the Church, *Lumen Gentium*, no. 6.

spiritual, Christ-centered nourishment of the people. It isn't primarily a commitment to the pastor's, the parish's, or the Church's financial stability.

4. The Good Shepherd knows his sheep personally and they know him (see John 10:14). It has been part of the Church's pastoral commitment that pastors have manageably sized parishes so that they can get to know each member of their flock personally, but this is not always possible given the shortage of priests. When we get involved in the ordinary lives of people and know them personally, we genuinely "smell like the sheep," as Pope Francis said. It is then that we know them and they know us.

   In addition, the Good Shepherd does not pick the wealthy over the poor or the poor over the wealthy. He aspires to know them all. The Code of Canon Law number 529 (paragraphs 1 and 2) emphasizes this need for pastors to strive to know the faithful entrusted to his care. One of the ways to do this is by visiting families, sharing in their joys and sorrows, and strengthening and enlightening them as the case may be, just like the pastor in our opening story. This is why it is vital to pray for more vocations. As the Book of Matthew said, "The harvest is rich, but the laborers are few" (9:37). With a growing need for good pastors and the ever-increasing shortage of priests, it is difficult to know every member of the parish personally. This does not make for very effective shepherding.

5. The Good Shepherd's sheep know and heed his voice (see John 10:4 and 16). Because the Good Shepherd's love and sacrifice are so impactful, the sheep heed the shepherd's voice. The grace of Christ, the Good Shepherd, makes this possible too. However, the shepherd has to be a voice of love and care so that the sheep will hear and listen. What inspires people the most is not sympathy but the realization

that they are cared for and loved. Love, mercy, empathy, and compassion inspire.

6. The Good Shepherd models the way for the sheep, and they follow (see John 10:4). The role of the shepherd as a leader is highlighted. The shepherd models the way. He leads by example and not merely by words. Actions, they say, speak louder than words. The Lord Jesus Christ himself walks the talk. To follow the example of Christ, the shepherd has to walk the talk. He has to mirror what he preaches in the Word and what he celebrates in the sacraments. Thanks be to God, who makes this possible by Christ's grace and our cooperation with that grace.

   When the sheep see the role-modeling life of the shepherd, they are more inclined to follow and to emulate the shepherd. People want to see Christ in the words and actions of their pastors. Even in the pastors' vulnerabilities and weaknesses, as we all are human, they want to see the way back to Christ, not away from Christ.

7. The Good Shepherd's mission is safety and life for the sheep (see John 10:10). The Lord says he comes so that we may have the fullness of life—salvation. The pastor's primary role is to see that God's people receive the grace of salvation, the fullness of life in Christ. Through preaching, the celebration of the sacraments, and the involvement in social affairs and social justice, this central goal is the driving force of good shepherding.

   On this Good Shepherd Sunday, we pray that Christ, the Good Shepherd, will inspire all the ministers of the Word and the sacraments. May we follow the example of Christ, the Good Shepherd. May the Lord inspire more people to open their hearts to the invitation of the pastoral vocation. Amen.

REFLECT

On this special day of prayer for vocations, it would be a beautiful thing to light a candle and pray for the priests who minister in my church or community or those for whom I feel the burden to pray. Will I do this? How may I encourage my ministers to be good shepherds?

PRAY

Lord, grant healing to wounded shepherds. Strengthen them and continue to inspire those you have chosen to minister in your Church. Amen.

Sunday, Year C

Hear, Listen, Believe, and Act

Readings: Acts of the Apostles 13:14,43–52;
Revelation 7:9,14b–17; John 10:27–30

I reflect on the Lord's message in John 10:27: "My sheep hear my voice, and I know them, and they follow me."

This passage reminds me of a contemporary story about a woman who went on a pilgrimage to the Holy Land. She observed how the sheep and the shepherds in Bethlehem interacted.

She watched the shepherds put their respective flocks in the same cave, the sheep intermingling. Wondering how the shepherds would ever be able to separate this sea of sheep, she rose early the next morning to observe. She watched while one of the shepherds walked some distance from the cave and beckoned his sheep, who ran out to him. The sheep knew the shepherd's voice. Together, shepherd and sheep went on their way.

Hearing the voice of the Shepherd—Christ—involves hearing, listening, believing, and doing; it is a progression from mere sensory receptivity to moral and spiritual transformation. In theological terms, it's the obedience of faith. Many are models of this faith.

Abraham hears, listens, believes, and acts upon the Word of God, as does Samuel, the other prophets, the apostles, and many heroes and heroines of our faith today. In the Holy Family of Nazareth, we see a family who hears, listens, believes, and acts.

The process of hearing can come in different ways. It might come through a direct reading of the Word of God at liturgy, it

85

might come privately, or it might come accidentally, as it did for Saint Augustine before he paid attention to it. It could also come as it did for Edith Stein, who was gripped by the power of the Word to declare, "This is the truth." It could even come as it did for Saint Ignatius of Loyola. He was used to reading romantic and, many times, indecent literature. But when indecent books weren't available for him to read while he was recouping from his leg surgery in 1521, he was stuck with what was available. He read the *De Vita Christi* by Ludolph of Saxony, which introduced him to contemplate the life of Jesus in Scripture.

We should be able to put ourselves in the "Zone of the Word of God." Affording ourselves the opportunity of hearing the Word of God is always a family builder, a vocation nurturer, and a grace-filling experience. The essential aspect of this "zone" is in the worshipping community, the Church.

"The call of God comes to us by means of a mediation that is communal. God calls us to become a part of the Church. After we have reached a certain maturity within it, he bestows on us a specific vocation. The vocational journey is undertaken together with the brothers and sisters whom the Lord has given to us; it is a convocation."[5]

Ask yourself: have you ever, as a family, opened your Bible and had a family sharing of God's Word? Have you ever shared the message contained in the Sunday readings or reflected together on the Sunday message? What kind of words and music do you share?

With what kind of message do you entertain yourself?

I remember growing up as a child and listening to my parents share their understanding of the Sunday reading; it was always an enriching experience.

---

5. Pope Francis, Message on the Occasion of the 53rd World Day of Prayer for Vocations.

I will stretch the act of hearing further by stressing listening. Listening has to do with paying attention to what we hear. Some may hear and not pay attention to what is heard. A typical example is the child who is getting ready for her first date while her mom reminds her of her school take-home assignment or the priest whose congregation consists of a bunch of kids compelled by their parents to go to Mass.

Listening is a choice. It takes the form of a study in some cases. Hopefully, we want to know more. We must pay attention to the Word of God because in it there is life. What we listen to may well impact what we believe.

Believing what we hear is crucial as well. We must welcome the Word we hear and allow it to be the center of our lives. We must allow the Word to take flesh. It is not just a question of intellectual acceptance but also of lived experience. For example, socialized marriage occurs when people marry in the Church simply because of compliance to social norms that are devoid of spiritual understanding of the Sacrament. Socialized priesthood occurs when a young man enters the priesthood for fame, money, and an extravagant lifestyle, all of which are wrong intentions, a condition of solemnity without awareness of the sanctity and grace being celebrated.

There is transforming power in the Word of God. By believing in the Word of God, we make ourselves beneficiaries of its transforming power. You cannot believe the Word of God without it having an impact in your life. There is an idea-motive dimension to the Word of God.

REFLECT

In my personal life, how do I create a welcome space for God's word? How often do I listen when I pray for God to show me how to serve? Do I open my heart to a more profound encounter with God? When was the last time I read my Bible?

> **PRAY**
> Lord Jesus Christ, give me the grace to discover my vocation, and when I do, give me the right disposition to say "Yes." Open my ears to hear you as you whisper. Amen.

Monday

Dealing with Discrimination

Readings: Acts 11:1–18; John 10:1–10

*D*o you want to know how the early Church handled the issue of discrimination? Read Acts of the Apostles, chapters 10–15. There you will find how the Christian mission knocks down the walls of hostility among people, providing opportunities for true reconciliation with God. In Saint Paul's words, "Christ has broken down the walls of hostility" (Ephesians 2:14).

In taking action against discrimination, the early Church is decisive. For example, Saint Peter, the leader of the Church and the first Pope, doesn't mince words in stating the inclusive and universal mission of the Church. He fights vehemently against those who think Christianity is a tribal religion. We find the story in Acts 10, but Peter uses it as a defense against discrimination in Acts 11:1–18. Saint Paul is at the forefront of this fight as well.

In the famous story of the vision God shows Peter concerning unclean animals, the Lord asks him to kill and eat the animals. Peter objects on religious grounds: "I have never eaten anything unclean." God replies, "You shall not call unclean what I have cleaned" (Acts 11:9).

Peter demonstrates that he understands this message when three men from Caesarea ask him to visit the family of Cornelius, a gentile. Recall that many Jews at the time do not socialize with gentiles for religious and cultural reasons, yet Peter doesn't hesitate and goes with the men. In Cornelius's house, the Holy Spirit descends on the gentiles just as the Holy Spirit descends on the disciples on the day of Pentecost. Saint Peter understands the gentiles are equally chosen as "we were" though they aren't Jewish.

This story sheds light on the universal mission of Christianity. It equally reveals how we should relate to each other as believers. Many times, we carry our tribal, ethnic, or cultural sentiments into our worship of God. We allow those to cloud, if not contaminate, the purity of our fellowship. Many times, we do not let the Holy Spirit break the walls of hostility and discrimination between us. However, whenever we do, there is much healing and peace.

There is freedom in seeing people for who they are as people, not for the color of their skin. It saves a lot of anxiety and stress. Relating to each other as God's children is the way Jesus has called us to live. It is the most healthy way. It is holy too.

Once, as I finished ministering to a group of people, a woman walked up to me and said, "God has used you to heal me of the wounds of hate I have carried for years. A black man abused my daughter, and I have since developed deep-seated hatred for people of color and shudder whenever I see a black man. As I came in for this seminar and the talks went on, I felt God renewing my heart, bringing healing to my wounds. Thank you for being the agent of my healing." Still in tears, she hugged me.

I'll bet she had never shaken the hand of a person of color after the terrible thing that happened to her daughter, let alone had a prolonged sobbing hug with a person of color. God bless her. I pray for healing for all in similar situations.

There is freedom in breaking down the walls of racial discrimination and all forms of discrimination—tribal, ethnic, cultural, class, and political—that cause hostility.

May this message bring us peace and freedom as we live the message of freedom available for all in Christ, the Good Shepherd, who laid down his life for many. Amen.

REFLECT

As a believer, how do I live the message of the gospel of inclusion? Do I discriminate against others because they are not like I am? Do I consider myself superior to another person?

PRAY

Lord, make me a messenger of the Good News of human equality. May I treat others with equal respect and dignity as your children. Amen.

Tuesday

Set Apart

Readings: Acts 11:19–26; John 10: 22–30

*B*elievers in the Lord Jesus are called two names in Acts of the Apostles. The first is "The Way," and the second is "Christians."

If you think those names are beautiful or intended to be complimentary, you are wrong. They are derogatory of the people who follow Christ.

"The Way" describes a movement, an unwelcome movement. The phrase appears about six times in Acts of the Apostles (see Acts 9:2, 19:9, 23; 22:4; 24:14, and 22). The first time this phrase appears is when Saul (Paul) asks the high priest for permission to hunt members of "The Way" and bring them as prisoners to Jerusalem.

The second name, which has come to stick, is "Christians." This name is given to Christians in Antioch because they are followers of Christ (see Acts 11:26). As a title, this word is used only two other times, in Acts 26:28 and in 1 Peter 4:16.

Why are believers called members of "The Way" and "Christians"? We may not fully know, but based on biblical and historical evidence, we can arrive at some conclusions.

There is something about believers in the Lord Jesus that makes them stand out. They are seen as different, as well as people on the fringe of society and power because of their way of life and the uniqueness of their worship. For outside observers, members of the early Church have a different way of life. Their faith is their unique way of life.

It is their core identity, and it makes them rare, separate from the rest. It is a New Way.

The story at Antioch is similar. Antioch was the third largest commercial city in ancient Rome, with a population of about half a million. It was the center of sports and entertainment. It was founded by Seleucus Nicator around 300 BC, who named it after his father, Antiochus. It was also the home of the temple of Daphne. Known as the goddess of sensual pleasure, she was worshipped by the people. Prostitution by her prophetesses was part of worshipping this goddess. It is in this city that the members of "The Way" are first called "Christians."

Why? Because these believers are different. Their understanding of worship, pleasure, social life, and sexual life is unlike the culture in which they live. Unlike many at Antioch, they are not part of the immorality that stamps the city. They are not like others in the pursuit of pleasure and self-gratification. They believe in the fidelity of marriage and the sacredness of sexual intimacy. They are also seen as a group of people who worship in a bizarre and utterly distinct way. Antiochians can see and identify them, not because of their racial or language differences, but because of their moral excellence and purity of creed. In reality, many of the early followers are native speakers of Greek and do not have a Jewish accent.

In *Mere Christianity*, the English writer C. S. Lewis writes extensively about the distinctive identity of Christians, part of which is their moral and creedal excellence and more of which is their profoundly renewed individual life.

Christianity is consistent with her calling when believers do not want to be like the world, not in the sense of biological endowments but in their morality and spiritual lives. We lose our identity if we no longer shine the light for everyone to see. The light must be the light of purity and unconditional love. It has to embrace the true sacredness of reproductive actions, honesty, and integrity. In short, it is the call to holiness, set apart and modeled after Christ.

If you are a Catholic, be bold. Be Christian. Be Catholic. There should be no in between.

> **REFLECT**
> As a Catholic, how proud am I of my faith? How proud am I to be a Christian?
>
> **PRAY**
> Lord Jesus, give me the grace to be the light of the world and the salt of the Earth. Amen.

Wednesday

First Things First

Readings: Acts 12:24–13:5a; John 12:44–50

*T*here is much to learn from the life of the early Church. The inspired writing in Acts of the Apostles is an excellent resource. I have been drawing from these lessons for the past two weeks. The following ideas are taken from Acts 13:1–3. Permit me to quote this passage:

"Now in the Church at Antioch, there were prophets and teachers, Barnabas, Symeon, who was called Niger, Lucius of Cyrene, Manaen a member of the court of Herod the tetrarch, and Saul. While they were worshiping the Lord and fasting, the Holy Spirit said, 'Set apart for me, Barnabas and Saul for the work to which I have called them.'

Then, completing their fasting and prayer, they laid hands on them and sent them off" (Acts 13:1–3).

The organizational structure of the early Church is simple. This is understandable because there were only a few thousand believers then. Similarly, the bulk of the Church's activity happens around Jerusalem, Antioch, and a few other Roman territories in proximity to Jerusalem.

I want to focus on how the early Church commissions missionaries and the serious way in which they take the work of evangelization. Observe how they are "worshiping the Lord and fasting" when the Holy Spirit speaks. Did you equally notice that even after the Holy Spirit speaks and Paul and Barnabas are selected for the first missionary journey, fasting and prayer occur before they are commissioned?

The Church is wise in her preparation of those who are to be ordained deacons or priests. It takes years of rigorous training focused around four dimensions known as the four pillars of priestly formation: human, spiritual, intellectual, and pastoral and apostolic. Each of these has several values plus competencies and skills. There is also a canonical requirement for a retreat preceding ordination. Besides all this, there are annual retreats designed to deepen the personal spiritual life of those who are discerning, especially seminarians. The intention is for candidates to be well grounded in a Christ-centered way of life, to be attuned to pastoral zeal and sensitivities, to love the Church, and to minister with fervor. Candidates are reminded continuously to be well rooted in the person of Christ as their core and priority. At least, this is a key objective.

Those called to the religious life go through a similar process of canonical retreat before their vows. Unfortunately, the all-important sacrament of matrimony does not have this long preparation. This is why I advise people discerning marriage to have a prayer time to ask the Lord to lead them all the way through.

Having said this about the vocations of service—holy orders and marriage—let me apply the same principle to our daily lives as believers. Often, we make decisions and then call God in after setting our minds on what we want to do. I propose the Christian model should be to ask God's guidance from the conception stage to the actual execution of the plan.

Those involved in ministry especially need to take this approach. From time to time, we run the Church as a business enterprise or as managers of a for-profit venture. We design a strategy, feel right about it, and go ahead and implement it. Hardly do we let God lead us in the process. Rarely do we immerse ourselves in the prayerful spirit of ministry by inviting the Holy Spirit to help us brainstorm, plan, and implement. We tend to forget we are ministers—shepherds—called to continually be in touch with Christ, the Good Shepherd, through prayers and fasting.

Granted, we have to be attentive to the business side to pay the bills. It is necessary to do so. Nevertheless, when business is the principal driver of our commitments in the Church, we have completely missed the point. In the long run, we lose. Nobody comes to Church to learn how to build business empires or be mentored into one for that matter. Business schools have that all covered. People come to Church to be spiritually fed and renewed. The Church is more vibrant when we do just that—minister the Word and the sacraments, bind the wounds, revive the spirits, and shine the light of Christ.

It is our blessing to invite God before, during, and after any mission we want to undertake as believers. It is our blessing to work with the Holy Spirit, leading by our knees first. This is the Christian way of doing things. It saves us from doing our own thing instead of allowing God to be the boss. You know that when God is in charge, we are at our best.

Thursday

Passionate about the Mission

Readings: Acts 13:13–25; John 13:16–20

We continue to glean inspiring resources from the early Church. Here, I look at how Saint Paul and his companions (Barnabas and John Mark, at least) continue the work of evangelization during their first missionary journey (see Acts 13:13–25).

They sail from Seleucia to Salamis, a reasonably large city and prominent seaport in Cyprus. As they travel, they preach the Good News of Christ and the Resurrection. Cyprus is the birthplace of Barnabas (see Acts 4:36). From Salamis of Cyprus, they trek their way to the Island of Paphos. They preach there also as they travel.

In Paphos, just like in many of the places they go, God confirms their words with incredible miracles of healing and conversion. Recall that it is in Paphos that they have a special invitation from the governor of the island. He is accompanied by Elymas, the magician, sorcerer, and false prophet. The power of the truth of the gospel from Saint Paul cannot stand the falsehood of the magician who does everything to confuse the governor from being open to the Good News. Saint Paul prays. The magician becomes blind in the process (see Acts 13:6–12), offering the governor clarity of vision to welcome the Good News.

From Paphos, Paul and his companions sail to Perga in Pamphylia. John Mark leaves them there and returns to Jerusalem. His departure, as we know from later documentation, hurts Saint Paul, but he later reconciles with him. From Perga, Paul and Barnabas go to Antioch in Pisidia. They are also given the invitation to preach in the synagogue. They do so (see Acts 13:13–25) with incredible power.

Again, every step of the way, they are ministering the word of God, sharing boldly and joyfully the Good News of saving grace. They pray with and for the people in synagogues, homes, and street centers and corners. They socialize with the people. Through the power of the risen Lord, God continues to confirm their works.

They are not on a cruise or vacation trip. They are not like adventurers who simply want to receive the blessings of nature and interact with new territories and cultures they meet. Rather, they are giving back the greatest news of hope, salvation, and grace everywhere they go. They are living the maxim of coming not to receive but to give, of being responsible stewards of the truth they have received that must be shared for others to benefit. They do not hold back any of the good things they receive from the Lord. In their bones, they know that if you receive something good, such as the Good News of saving grace, it has to be spread. These are ideas worth sharing, worth telling from the mountaintop.

This is an excellent lesson for us, the so-called believers of today. If Saint Paul and his companions were alive today, I'll bet they would be everywhere. They would be in every social media outlet and in every space from where you can reach people. They would not settle for the security and comfort of air-conditioned churches, parish offices, and locked-in membership registers. They would be sharing their faith testimonies and not settling for old membership. They would be spreading the ideas that change the world.

How about tapping from the apostolic zeal of the early Church?

REFLECT
How passionate am I about the gospel? In what ways am I sharing the Good News? What news do I share in social media?

PRAY
O Holy Spirit, kindle in me the passion and love for the Good News. May I joyfully and boldly share it as my life's story. Amen.

Friday

Let Not Your Hearts Be Troubled

Readings: Acts 13:26–33; John 14:1–6

Waiting rooms at heart hospitals are an anxious place to be. As families and friends wait for the news after a loved one has had a heart attack, the dominant mood is nothing to be desired. Ominous faces. Sad looks. Depressing spirits. Long silences.

"Is she going to be okay?" "Is everything going to be all right?" "How soon will we know?" Questions fly back and forth. In the meantime, some who may not have prayed in a long time dust their Bibles, rosaries, or other religious items and struggle to lift their hearts in prayer. Waiting for the news after a heart attack is always tense.

Why is this the case? One of the reasons may be the gripping power of the potential sudden end of life. Not even the stoics, those ancient philosophers who act as if they have no emotions, could stand the volatility of such an unpredictable outcome. One's state of mind can be all over the place when confronted with the power of death or a sudden change in a loved one's health.

Suppose the cardiologist comes with good news: "We caught it in time, and after a few surgeries, she will be okay." Faces brighten. Smiles appear.

If the news isn't so good, the doctor says, "It's a rare case. I advise you to keep hope alive while we do our best." Faces drop. You will observe family and friends holding onto different sources of hope.

Perhaps, providentially, a fellow patient walks out of the clinic after his routine check-up and notices the somber faces of the family. He decides to find out what is going on. At first, nobody will talk, but when they realize he is a heart attack survivor, they open up to him.

He seems more positive than the picture of doomsday the family is painting. Gradually, he takes charge of the discussion, explaining details of his highly complicated case and how, by sheer hope, trust in God, and the doctors' expertise, he lived to tell about it.

Hearing this, the faces of the listening family members brighten. The witness of this survivor is reassuring. At least they know, firsthand, it's possible their family member will survive.

Think about this kind of scenario. I have seen it over and over again in the past two decades. You may have been a witness to similar situations too. As you think about the story, reflect on the Gospel of John 14:1–6. The Lord Jesus reassures his disciples: "Let not your heart be troubled, believe in God, also believe in me" (John 14:1).

The disciples are worried he is leaving them. They are afraid he has predicted the betrayals against him. They are concerned about what will become of their hope in his messiahship. They are worried about so many other things, just as many of us are worried about health, food, bills, the pandemic, the future, and so on. Some are also deeply sad. They wonder, "When can we return to Mass and receive the Lord in communion?"

The ultimate answer to human worries comes from the one who has been there before us and has returned to tell us the Good News. The answer is faith in God, faith in Christ, belief in God. Faith in Christ as the Savior, the Way, the Truth, and the Life is key to victory. It is triumphantly journeying on the wings of providence amidst our worries. There is sufficient room for us in God, where we can rest.

REFLECT
Do I tap from the encouraging value of my faith when I am worried? Do I realize my faith in Christ is strong enough to carry me when everything seems to be falling apart?

PRAY
I'm praying for blessed assurance in moments of despair. May the same favor be granted to those who are despairing right now. Amen.

Saturday

Reroute!

Readings: Acts 13:44–52; John 14:7–14

*H*ave you observed how trickles of water flow from rocks in a creek? The water follows different paths but merges into a spring, a lake, a river, or an ocean. For the most part, the water flows through rough and twisted tracks.

You will observe that as the water trickles from the rock, it bypasses the stumbling blocks, those rocks or pieces of wood that stand in the way. Though the rocks or wood remain stationary, they do not stop the stream from flowing. Instead, the stream's navigation is made even more colorful and scenic as it flows around the stumbling blocks.

One may learn from the navigation of streams the secret to thriving amidst stumbling blocks. Often, people are concerned they have few opportunities to succeed due to stumbling blocks along the way. It appears that in living God's Word in particular, there are many stumbling blocks. Some wonder how to deal with this reality.

A man once complained that there was no sense of spiritual direction in his parish and that anyone who tried to help fan the flame of divine love and service was opposed by people who felt they owned the parish.

Some people say they can't seem to see the end of the tunnel. They forget that the end of the tunnel only yields insight when we are close to it. Until then, it seems the way is unattainable.

How about seeing stumbling blocks as pieces of wood in the path of flowing water? Fortunately, those stumbling blocks are opportunities for the beautiful scenic road to become fruitful in service.

Right from the time of the New Testament until now, no work of evangelization, work of charity, or act of faith in the Lord and Savior Jesus Christ has been without stumbling blocks. For example, read Acts of the Apostles 13:44–46. The jealousy, backbiting, and opposition against Paul and Barnabas during their first missionary journey warrants them to reroute and channel their mission to the gentiles. Also, the Lord tells the disciples that when they are persecuted in one place to move to another (see Matthew 10:23).

Refocus.

You may have heard the saying that when one door closes, another opens. For the believer, there are no closed doors. Instead, there are paths to better doors. There are many doors out there for you to find peace and joy. There are many doors out there beckoning your service. Do not be stuck or allow yourself to be held hostage by the roadblocks of naysayers.

Hear the apostles speak about their change of plans: "The word of God needed to be spoken first to you. Since you reject it and judge yourselves to be unworthy of eternal life, we are now turning to the Gentiles" (Acts 13:44–46).

Don't you realize that a stumbling block on your path to doing God's will doesn't mean the end of the road? It merely means there are many other alternatives, even better alternatives you wouldn't otherwise know.

Great evangelizers love stumbling blocks, not that they seek them out. Instead, they dare them, look them straight in the eye, and walk past them. True believers overcome roadblocks. Roadblocks don't deter them. The saints cherish roadblocks because, through them, the limits of their courage and vision to be the best God has called them to be expand.

Therefore, do not lament an unsuccessful attempt. Do not lie down and throw a pity party. Do not act the victim. Look and see: God is calling you to reroute to the path you need most now. Refocus. See the road. Follow it.

REFLECT

When I meet roadblocks on my path to progress, do I get stuck or do I see them as divine opportunities to pray, create, and refocus? Have I discovered the power of determination, faith, and bigger dreams? How may I let God lead me to better ways of doing this and other things?

PRAY

My Lord and my God, lead me through the hurdles I face. May I see what you want to show me in roadblocks and discover a better path to blessings. Amen.

WEEK FIVE OF EASTER

Sunday, Year A

The Way, the Truth, and the Life

Readings: Acts 6:1–7; 1 Peter 2:4–9; John 14:1–12

*S*aint Augustine, the Doctor of Grace (354–430 AD), who was from Thagaste Numidia, modern-day Algeria in North Africa, provides a brilliant line in his beautiful sermon on John 14:6. He notes that every human being desires truth and life but "not every person finds the way to truth and life."[6] This line is an excellent introduction to a reflection on Jesus Christ as the way, the truth, and the life.

Consider that all of us desire life and truth. The search for the truth and fullness of life is at the core of everything we aspire and do. The baby crawling toward a toy desires life just as senior citizens wishing the best for their families desire life. Universities, hospitals, shopping malls, and theaters, in one way or another, exist to satisfy the desire or, should I say, the need for life, fullness of life, and truth.

---

6. Augustine of Hippo (1888), "Sermons on Selected Lessons of the New Testament" in P. Schaff (Ed.), R. G. McMullen (Tans, *Saint Augustine Sermon on the Mount, Harmony of the Gospel, Homilies on the Gospels*, vol. 6, (New York: Christian Literature Company), p. 531.

Enduring happiness is a life lived to the fullest. Discovering the truth is a delight for the soul.

However, the way to the truth and fulfilled life is what many argue about and find hard to discover. It is an age-old struggle. But the Lord makes a daring proclamation to his disciples as well as to us: "I am the Way" (John 14:6).

There seems to be a consensus among biblical scholars that the emphasis of John 14:6 is on "the way." Hence B. M Newman and E. A. Nida in *A Handbook on the Gospel of John* re-rendered the text to read, "I am the way that reveals the truth [about God] and gives life to people."[7]

I believe this revelation contains one of the distinguishing marks of Christianity and Jesus as the Savior. We do not do justice to Jesus' claim if we do not take this and analyze it in its own right. Rarely do Scripture scholars agree on any given biblical text, but regarding John 14:6, there seems to be consensus that the meaning as translated in various English versions is consistent with the words of Jesus and the original language of the biblical text.

Jesus adds to this revelation by saying, "No one can come to the Father except through me" (John 14:6b). In other words, the Lord Jesus says that "All people must go to the father by me" or "I am the only road that leads to the father."[8]

It's important to note that no religious founder claims to be the way, the truth, and the life; nor do any claim to have absolute access to God the Father. And we must be fair to represent who they say they are and what they say their mission is.

For instance, in researching Gautama Buddha, we notice that having found "enlightenment," he wrote an ethical code for anyone who wants to discover "truth and life." He never claimed he is the

7. Barclay Moon Newman and Eugene Albert Nida, *A Handbook on the Gospel of John*, UBS Handbook Series (New York: United Bible Societies, 1993), p. 457.

8. Ibid.

way to enlightenment "or the truth and life." To attribute such a title to him is to lie against him and the respected tradition of Buddhism.

Confucius' humility and self-awareness are evident in his testimonial about himself. He said, "I have not been able to practice virtue aright . . . I have not been able to utter or pursue aright what I have learned . . . I have been unable to change that which was wrong. These are my sorrows . . . In knowledge, perhaps I am equal to other men, but I have not been able to transform the essence of what is noble into deed." I love his humility and honesty.

Mohammad, the revered founder of Islam, didn't claim what he is not either. Towards the end of his life, despite his military conquests and successes, he admitted how sinful and in need of mercy he was, just like all of us. "Fearful, beseeching, seeking for shelter, weak and in need of mercy," he said. "I confess my sins before thee, presenting my supplication as the poor supplicate the rich." He addressed his prayer to God (Allah in his language). Mohammad never claimed to be the way; neither did he claim to be the truth and the life.

Between Buddha and Confucius and Mohammad, the founders of three of the four world's largest religions, there is a thread. We can see genuine humility and an acknowledgment of their identities as humans in search of the truth and life. None claimed to be the way, the truth, and the life. Only Jesus does.

Upon this fact, therefore, lies the authenticity, integrity, or falsehood of Jesus' claim. It must either be true or false. If it is true, then we should respond to it with the moral responsibility required of the truth. If it is false, then the entire claim of Jesus can be completely thrown in the trashcan. Here the famous words of C. S. Lewis in *Mere Christianity* are apt: "Jesus was either a liar or a lunatic or the Lord."

If it is true, then Jesus states that we do not need to second guess the way to life in God and the truth, who is God. He is the answer, the full package, we seek.

I believe. I follow him, the way to life and truth.

REFLECT

As a baptized Christian and Catholic, how convinced am I that Jesus is my Lord and Savior? How confident am I about his divinity? How would I explain this to anyone who asks?

PRAY

I pray that I may continue to discover Jesus Christ as Lord and deepen my relationship with him, who is one with the Father and the way to him. Amen.

Sunday, Year B

Fruitfulness in Christ

Readings: Acts 9:26–31; 1 John 3:18–24; John 15:1–8

*I*n this reflection, I share three of the keys to fruitfulness in ministry.

I have had the privilege of ministering in many organizations, parishes, and ministries, some in Africa and others in North America and Europe. One of the biggest concerns of leaders in various ministries and faith-based organizations is fruitfulness.

Dioceses, parishes, and church ministries and organizations are concerned about how to grow our Church and ministry and inspire more lives to know the Lord. This need is ever more evident, given that the Christian message is becoming less popular. Of course, believers should not be concerned about winning a popularity contest. That is not and never has been the way of the Lord. Remember how, when the people wanted to crown him king, he slipped away to be by himself (see John 6:15)? He does not wish such a route for his Body, the Church.

Since we are not in a popularity contest, how can we be effective in bearing witness to Christ and how do we become fruitful in ministry?

"Fruitful" is another way of saying "effective." In turn, effectiveness has to be understood as conversion and faith deepening. Growing in numbers and economic growth is simply an offshoot of growth in the faith of people. It is when people's lives are changed and they buy into the values of the gospel that they begin to invest their time, talent, and treasure to support it. Rarely do people invest in what they do not find valuable.

There are many insights from the tremendous pastoral works of the holy fathers, Paul VI (*Evangelii Nuntiandi*), John Paull II (*Redemptoris Missio*), and Francis (*Evangelii Gaudium*). There are many other insights in theological and spiritual literature.

I have read quite a few of these works, and they have been an asset, but most helpful of all is Scripture, especially the Lord's words throughout the time he is with his disciples. Here I draw from the lessons of the Gospel of John 15:1–8 and the testimony in Acts 9:26–31.

I can summarize the secret of effectiveness in ministry in its three most essential principles; upon these rest other human and leadership qualities we may bring to enrich the ministry. These three principles include a personal encounter with and profound love for Christ the Lord. In other words, we must remain in Christ's love. The Lord Jesus tells us that bearing fruits rests in loving him and the Father. When we do this, he sends us the Spirit. The Lord makes this teaching clear in John 14. I will share more on this theme in the reflection for Monday, Easter Week Five. It is connected with the second principle, namely abiding in Christ.

The Lord also tells us that fruitfulness lies in our abiding in him (John 15). The Lord emphasizes this organic relationship between fruitfulness and living in him by using the metaphor of the vine and the branches: "Abide in me, and I in you. As the branch cannot bear fruit by itself, unless it abides in the vine, neither can you, unless you abide in me" (John 15:4). The entire Gospel of John, chapter fifteen, flushes out this crucial aspect of the ministry's effectiveness.

The third principle is allowing the Holy Spirit to lead us. It means we have to welcome the Holy Spirit in our hearts and allow the Spirit to impregnate our lives and ministry. As the principal agent of the work of evangelization,[9] the Holy Spirit is the fruitful ministry's lifeline. Without the Holy Spirit, no life can be given to those to whom we minister.

---

9. Pope Paul VI, *Evangelii Nuntiandi*, no. 75.

See in the life and ministry of the newly converted Saint Paul how his personal encounter with the Lord and his newfound love become an inspiration for action. Moreover, we read that the early Church in Galilee and Samaria is built up and multiplied. The reason? The people have awe, reverence, for the Lord. It is rooted in their hearts. Also, they are led in "the comfort of the Spirit" (Acts 9:31).

Thus, here are my suggestions for the three most crucial principles to fruitfulness in ministry:

1. Be passionately in love with Christ and his body, the Church. This intense love is evident when we work with people or share the faith. If you aren't passionate about it, how do you expect other people to be?

2. Abide in Christ and the faith you have in the Lord. No matter what happens, tuck this treasure of knowing the Lord into your heart. Keep that faith in him as your Lord. Remain in his body.

3. Be in love with the Holy Spirit and allow the Spirit to lead you. It is the Spirit that gives life, not us. It is the spirit of Christ that is the grace that sustains the work and makes it bear fruit.

I hope these three fundamental principles help us discover more profound love and faith in Christ. Amen.

REFLECT

What things have I done that have been effective in bearing witness to the gospel? That time a believer's life impacted mine positively, what was it about the person that touched me the most? In what ways can I grow in the love of God in Christ and allow the Holy Spirit to lead me?

PRAY

O Holy Spirit, you are the lifeline of success in spiritual life and ministry. I welcome you to my life. I need your anointing to love the Lord more and love his body with great affection to bear testimony to this love with great passion. Amen.

Sunday, Year C

New Heaven, New Earth, and the New Jerusalem

Readings: Acts 14: 21–27; Revelation 21:1–5a; John 13:31–33a, 34–35

*M*any of us are familiar with NASA's Apollo program that made headlines in the 1960s for its voyage around the moon. The responses by religious denominations that were very upset with NASA were intriguing. Representatives of various churches, very religious people, said the space program must be a sham. Why? Because the Apollo astronauts circled the moon and landed on it but did not report they had found the New Jerusalem.

These denominations were fundamentalist in their word-for-word literal interpretation of the Bible. They were convinced the New Jerusalem had to be up in the sky somewhere, waiting to come down. They were upset because they thought NASA, having gone around the moon, was hiding the truth.

Is the New Jerusalem on the moon? Does it exist?

New Jerusalem does exist. Space, where God makes his home among humanity, is real. It's the place where his name is Emmanuel— God with us. God's City, the New Jerusalem, is begun right here. His city on Earth is the Church.

By "Church," I don't mean the buildings and edifices of beautiful cathedrals. By "Church," I mean this: *ekklesia tou theou, en Kristo,* the Assembly of God in Christ. I mean the people of God, united in love with Jesus Christ and empowered by the Holy Spirit. The Church is the people of God, their human hearts renewed by the Spirit of the living God. The Church is the means of communication from Christ to other people, the sacrament of Christ's love among people. The Church is united in one faith, one love, and the sacraments. The Church is holy because of the holiness of Christ, universal and flowing from the living tradition of the apostles.

Saint Augustine of Hippo writes beautifully about this New Jerusalem in *The City of God.* The starting point of this new people is faith in Christ, faith, as it is believed, lived, proclaimed, and practiced in the Church and expressed by charity. The Lord Jesus says, "This is how all will know you are my disciples: your love for one another" (John 13:35). Those who are thus born anew in Christ become witnesses of Christ to others.

People encounter Christ in people who continue his life. The underground Church, under Communist persecution, met Christ by the love shared by believers. Numerous Indian poor encountered Christ in Mother Teresa of Calcutta. In the 2010 Haiti earthquake, victims encountered Christ through Christian charities. These disciples, living in union with Christ and making his presence a reality in the world, are the New Jerusalem. These people are the Church. Jesus Christ becomes one of us so we may see, hear, touch, and be fully exposed to God's love among us. His Spirit unites his people into a single family, the Family of God, the Church.

The New Jerusalem is the transformation of the world into the Body of Christ. Under this body, love takes a different dimension: "Love one another as I have loved you" (John 13:34). In this assembly, people live in love and share their love in a self-sacrificing way.

We, the members of the New Jerusalem, have the deepest of responsibilities in the world. We must render Christ present for others in the way we love them and in the way we love each other.

Love is not just something we do. Love, loving the way Christ loved, sacrificial love, is how we express the essence of our beings as Christians.

It's how we shine the light of Christ to the world. It should be who we are, who we have become, in Christ.

The world needs the witness of this love. The world needs Christ. And he can be found in the New Jerusalem, among the People of God, united in love in Christ under one head, one faith, one love, and one baptism.

> **REFLECT**
> In what ways am I Christ to others? Is my life a witness to the life of Christ where I live and work? How may I continue to be Christ to others as well as a resource for spiritual strengthening?
>
> **PRAY**
> I pray that I reveal Christ and am a witness of God's saving love in all I do. May I be a source of inspiration to others. Amen.

Alternative Reflection

Learning from Saint Paul

*Readings: Acts 14: 21–27; Revelation 21:1–5a;
John 13:31–33a, 34–35*

I share a lesson from Saint Paul's first missionary journey about being sources of strengthening for others.

In Acts 14:21–27, we read of Paul and Barnabas' missionary activities in Derbe and their return to the places (Lystra, Iconium, and Antioch) where they had earlier preached. Derbe is a remote border city in Galatia. Remember that, at the time, Galatia was a Roman City.

We notice two crucial actions Paul and Barnabas undertake in their missionary work as recorded in the above verses. They preach (Acts 14:21) as well as strengthen the believers (Acts 14:22).

These are crucial aspects of the work of evangelization. What do we do when we come to church on Sundays? We worship the Lord, don't we? We proclaim the gospel and preach or hear the sermons or homilies. We pray together and break bread in Holy Communion. In these actions, we hear God's Word inspire us. Sometimes, these words call us to a change of life, conversion, or ongoing conversion. Other times, they serve as an encouragement to confirm us in our faith.

Sometimes we ignore the aspect of strengthening because we pay so much attention to the conversion part. We evangelizers have to strengthen the faith of believers. They need inspiring words of hope so that they carry on.

In the world, many believers hear lots of depressing news. They are persecuted and put down. In churches, they should be lifted. They should be motivated. They should be inspired. Believers, wherever they find themselves, should be channels of this Christ-centered strengthening.

I would like us to see the role of the evangelizer as that of a coach. The coach inspires his players to discover their gifts and talents and to maximize their use.

We learn from Saint Paul both how to preach conversion unto Christ and how to strengthen the converted and believers. In our Catholic tradition, we call this faith deepening. In faith deepening, we shed more light on what we have received. We also inspire and strengthen believers to go deeper into the good things the Lord has given them.

We want them to become proudly Christian and proudly Catholic—in other words, proud believers. In order to hold their heads high and walk the talk of confident discipleship, we have to approach them from the position of spiritual strength. We have to be strengthened by the Lord and God's word. We have to be enthused.

REFLECT

What plan do I have for implementing the aspect of witnessing to Christ through strengthening others and confirming them in their faith? How am I or can I be a source of spiritual support for others?

PRAY

I pray that I may learn from Saint Paul how to be a witness of the love of God and how to be a channel of the strengthening power of the Holy Spirit. Amen.

Monday

God Revealed through the Believer

Readings: Acts 14:5–18; John 14:21–26

I reflect on the blessings of being Christ to others, an excellent gift for any true believer.

While on Earth, the Lord Jesus mentors his disciples on how they will be his witnesses. We read that the Lord speaks to them about how anyone who loves him and obeys his word will be God's special child. This person will receive the precious grace of divine life.

The Lord says, "My Father will love those who love me, and I will love them and reveal myself to them" (John 14:21, NRSV). He continues, "Those who love me will keep my word, and my Father will love them, and we will come to them and make our home with them . . . The Holy Spirit, whom the Father will send in my name, will teach you everything and remind you of all that I have said to you" (John 14:23, 25–26, NRSV).

Pause for a while and reflect on the blessings of God revealing himself to you. Imagine God making a home in your heart and entire being. This is amazing grace.

This promise is fulfilled in the early Church as it continues to be fulfilled today in the lives of true believers. In the case of Saint Paul during his first missionary journey, Christ reveals himself to him in his words and actions.

Take, for example, Paul's witness of life in Lystra. Lystra at the time was a small frontier created by the Roman emperor. It was said to be located in present-day Turkey. Saint Paul's words become life giving, and his presence reveals divine life.

Saint Paul speaks to a disabled person who is listening. His words, as one to whom Christ has revealed himself, carry the power of the risen Lord. They have the power to bring life to stifled muscles and dead cells. There is life, abundant life, in the words of anyone in whom Christ lives. There is power, resurrection power, manifested through the actions of the true believer. I see this around me. I witness it in churches and religious activities where faith is alive. God goes on working in the lives of true believers.

The local people from Lystra who aren't exposed to such manifestations of divine life in human persons mistake Paul and Barnabas for gods. The locals can't believe humans can be channels of divine healing and grace. They can't comprehend that Christ goes on working in the hearts and minds, words, and actions of true believers.

Similar to these locals are those who do not see and perceive that God continues working today in the lives of true believers. Even among believers, some doubt if Christ lives on in his body and members, the Church, today.

The Lord has promised, and his word is true, the following: "Truly, truly, I say to you, he who believes in me will also do the works that I do; greater works than these will he do because I go to the Father" (John 14:12).

I hope that you, as a believer, hold on to these words of Christ. Continue to be, by the grace of the Holy Spirit, the hands and feet of Jesus Christ. As another Christ, wherever you live, bring healing to the wounded. Reveal hope to the depressed. Bring comfort to the sorrowful. Be the Lord's shalom.

Tuesday

The Necessity of a Support System

Readings: Acts 14:19–28; John 14:27–31a

*A*n Igbo African proverb comes to mind this morning as I meditate on what happens to Saint Paul in Acts 14:19–20, which chronicles the famous story of his stoning. The proverb is this: "Anya bebe, imi bebe." It means, "What affects a member of the family affects another." The literal translation is, "When the eye is crying; the nose cries with it."

Suppose you are passing through a difficult time. It could be the loss of a loved one or a job. Or say you are a victim of an attack by a malicious clique simply because you want to do the right thing. Whatever the reason, you feel very low, and no one, no friend or church member, is a support system when you need it most. How do you feel?

Now, say a believer you admire shows up. Maybe it's a member of your morning prayer group who pays a surprise visit. The person prays with you, offers inspiring words, and makes you laugh. Now, how do you feel?

One of the precious symbols about the Church we learn from Saint Paul is that the Church is the Body of Christ. Christ is the head, and we are the members. What affects one member of the family affects the other. When one member is broken, others should feel the need to heal. We are a community. We are a family, the family of God. This is why we need to be a support system for one another.

If God were to open our eyes to see the power of a support system, we all would choose more of it. If we were to have insight into the power of solidarity in moments of need, it would heighten our urgency to bring the news of joy. I suppose all of us would hastily go to find someone we could help out of a depressing or trying situation.

Saint Paul is stoned and dragged out of the city by an opposition group in Lystra that thinks he is dead. I suggest the power of prayerful solidarity restores him to life. Hear how the Bible tells the story: "When the disciples gathered about him [Paul], he rose and entered the city, and on the next day, he went on with Barnabas to Derbe" (Acts 14:20).

Look around you. Many are knocked down and possibly on the verge of depression if not already depressed. It could be for lack of warmth, food, or clothing or because of neglect, hatred, or for any other reason. Many people walk out of the Church because nobody will say "Hello" and welcome them, even on a Sunday.

Would you please find someone today to make smile? Would you place a call to someone who might need it? Please look around your community and offer a spiritual helping hand to someone. You might also look in your church and find that person who is persecuted or ostracized because of their faith and let them know you care.

These simple gestures could warm hearts and awaken those who are knocked down.

> **REFLECT**
> Are there simple gestures of kindness and love I may do today
> and this week to help heal someone who is hurting? In what
> ways can I help the community in which I live heal from hate
> and violence?
>
> **PRAY**
> Lord, as you wished peace to your people, make me an instrument
> of peace and healing wherever I am. Amen.

Wednesday

Lessons from the First Christian Council (Part One)

Readings: Acts 15:1–6; John 15:1–8

The events of the Council of Jerusalem in 50 AD, also known as
the First Christian Council, are recorded in the Acts of the Apostles
15. What do they teach us about the leadership of the early Church?
What do we glean from them about Christianity in general? This is a
broad question, so I will shed light on a couple of ideas in this and
following reflections, focusing on prayerful engagement with the ideas
in the Word.

Many times, we begin a mission without being aware of its
implications. I remember when the Lord led me to evangelization

through television and other media here in the United States. Poor me from Africa. I didn't know that sooner or later I would have to hire attorneys, seek insights from consultants, and regularly call my bishop. Sometimes I even contracted with canonists who helped me do things the right way. Many of your works are probably like that; you jump into something without understanding what it entails.

Paul and Barnabas experience their fair share of this. The Holy Spirit calls them for a unique mission, which they realize is to preach to the gentiles (see Acts 13 and 14). Their preaching and miracles in Antioch, the Island of Cyprus, and Southwestern Asia Minor are fruitful and result in a massive influx of gentiles into the Church. This influx comes with a price, though.

Some Jews, who are the first to accept Christ, see the conversion of gentiles into Christianity as an incomplete if not half-baked idea. They think they must save Judaism from this contamination, or at least elevate Christian faith by adding more Jewish ritual. Thus, these zealots hurry to the headquarters of Paul's ministry in Antioch to teach the gentiles that Christian baptism is not sufficient to save them. They say they need Jewish circumcision too that comes with the observance of the Law of Moses. These Jews mean well even though their proposal goes against the core of the Christian view of salvation by grace.

Trust fiery Paul to not take this lightly. He engages these zealots and fiercely opposes their ideas. They claim top Church leadership in Jerusalem supports their teaching. In contrast, Paul and Barnabas insist this isn't consistent with the Church's teaching, and Paul demands they go back to the Church in Jerusalem to iron out the issue. The events of the council are recorded in Acts 15:1–35.

Lesson: from the beginning of the Church, the need for teaching authority is identified and practiced. Present at the council are the apostles (*espicopoi*) and the elders (presbyters), two names that are synonyms for bishops and priests. One could say that the debates and deliberations of the council involve the early theological testimonials. They live with Christ, hear him, and follow the unique path, a tradition he sets for them.

Isn't it reasonable to have a teaching authority? Through the grace of the Holy Spirit, right from the early days of the Church, the teaching authority maintains the tradition of the Church. Primarily exercised through the episcopal office, it offers an authentic interpretation of the Word of God in Scripture and tradition.

If nothing else, the surge of self-made prophets and pastors in social media and the ridiculous interpretations they make of the Bible reinforce the common-sense need for an authentic interpretation of Scripture. If interpreting the Bible and Christian tradition were left to my subjective whims and caprices, anything could pass for solid doctrine. I could propose a salvation thesis based on my personal taste or exclusive cultural values. The result could be a syncretistic Christianity, the kind these zealot converts to Christianity want. Thanks be to God we have the teaching authority, the magisterium.

In the next reflection, I will expand on other lessons we can learn from the First Christian Council.

REFLECT

How do I see the role of the teaching authority of the Church? Do I appreciate its relevance in guiding the faithful in the way of truth and safeguarding against error? How do I support the authority of the bishop of my local church through prayer and encouraging feedback when I have the opportunity?

PRAY

Lord, continue to lead the Church to tap from the wealth of your Word. Give me the grace of devout devotion to your Word. Amen.

Thursday

Lessons from the First Christian Council (Part Two)

Readings: Acts 15:7–21; John 15:9–11

I continue our reflection on the lessons from the First Christian Council that took place in Jerusalem around 50 AD. The main issue of deliberation among the early Church leaders was determining whether salvation depends on God's grace through faith in Jesus Christ or on circumcision and the practice of the Mosaic Law.

The most fundamental question is whether one needs to be a Jew or a member of a particular culture with specific rituals to be saved or if salvation comes through faith in Jesus Christ by God's grace.

Often, believers impose their cultural behaviors as a necessary part of the salvation package when it isn't. For instance, the Church encourages active participation at liturgy. This includes singing along when a song is intoned, but some cultures hardly sing unless accompanied by an instrument or choir. I come from Africa, where virtually everybody sings and dances, choir or no choir, but I shouldn't suppose that people from regions where singing is uncommon are not active at liturgy. The lesson is, it is spiritually beneficial to avoid imposing our cultural heritage as if it is a universal norm. The danger is religious syncretism that causes Christianity to lose its core identity.

I don't believe Paul and Barnabas would have objected if those enthusiasts had told the people they might be circumcised. There were and are many who are circumcised for reasons other than for salvation.

Like other councils that have come after this first one, the magisterial decision was primarily guided by two principles, all led by the Holy Spirit. First, what does Scripture say? Second, what do we discern from the tradition we have from when Christ preached and worked among us?

Remember, by the time of this council, no part of the New Testament was written. The only part of Scripture they had was the Old Testament. Still, their interpretation of tradition was enriched by the faith of the faithful, furnished by what they saw Jesus do and teach.

In the same way, Scripture and tradition are the two interlocking poles shaping any valid decision or interpretation the magisterium makes concerning faith and morals. It isn't merely opinion polls from individual bishops. As we know, the magisterium is at the service of Christ, the Word of God—the service of sacred Scripture and sacred tradition.[10]

Another lesson from the event of the council is that magisterial decisions do not necessarily end the controversy. History shows that some will continue to hold erroneous beliefs. The Council of Jerusalem did not stop the heretics. Some listened and understood. Others continued the fight; hence we had the first Christian sect called the Ebionites, though they became extinct over time.

Research the histories of the councils, from the first Ecumenical council called the First Council of Nicaea in 325 to the Second Vatican Council. No council has ended without camps divided between supporters and opponents, yet the Church remains strong.

REFLECT

When I am confronted with issues of debate in the Church, how do I take it? Do I want to prove a point, win the argument, or show a deep reverence for the truth of the gospel even if it

---

10. *Catechism of the Catholic Church*, no. 86.

is opposed to my personal preference? How disposed am I to honor God's word?

PRAY

Lord Jesus, keep your Church from heresies; bring unity to her members. Make me devoted to love your Word and the truth and show reverence to it. May I promote the truth, not an error. Guide me in your truth. Amen.

Friday

Lessons from the First Christian Council (Part Three)

Readings: Acts 15:22–31; John 15:12–17

I conclude the reflection centered on the lessons from the First Christian Council by commenting on the place of doctrine in our faith.

Nowadays, as it has been since the time of the Enlightenment, some people strongly object to a church shaped by doctrinal teachings. Some claim doctrine is a mere tool of the "institutional church" and is designed to restrict the free spirit of the gospel. Others suggest doctrine is pedantic and old-fashioned. They propose that a return to the true spirit of the gospel frees the faithful from doctrinal teachings. Nevertheless, we see from the experience of the early Church something different.

We read of the way and manner in which the early Church resolves the first debate about justification and salvation: by siding with Christ's standards and proposing to the gentiles that they don't need circumcision to be saved. Instead, the apostles and presbyters propose four things to avoid: abstaining from what has been sacrificed to idols, abstaining from blood, abstaining from strangled meat, and abstaining from unchastity (Acts 15:29). More importantly, I am captivated by how the message is presented to the gentile faithful. The apostles emphasize that "it has seemed good to the Holy Spirit and us to lay upon you no greater burden than is necessary" (Acts 15:28). This suggests the apostles were convinced that the Holy Spirit inspired their teaching. I believe their resolution was rooted in pure love for the faithful and the law of charity. They were concerned not to burden the faithful with what was unnecessary. Such teaching is consistent with the Christian core belief (dogma) regarding the law of charity. It is in line with the central mandate of love the Lord Jesus sets forth for his body, the Church (see John 15:12, 17).

Doctrine (*doctrina*) is simply the Latin word for teaching or instruction, and it appears about fifty-one times in the New Testament. It comes from the Greek διδαχή (*didache*), or, more specifically, relating to apostolic teachings, from διδασκαλία (*didaskalia*), which also means teaching or instruction. There is much more to the use of these concepts beyond my expertise; Biblical and Scripture experts and linguists are more equipped to delve into such specificities.

However, in simple terms, one could say that doctrine is the codification or the summary of the core beliefs of any institution, in this case the Church. The core beliefs could be described as dogma. So, doctrines are the teachings of the dogmas of a faith tradition. In our Christian faith, this is the condensed version of our faith designed for teaching and instructional purposes.

One of the Church's earliest documents, which systemized the way the Eucharist was celebrated in the first century of the Church, was titled *Didache*. The long title is about the "Lord's teaching through the Twelve Apostles to the nations" (gentiles). These teachings were praxis-oriented doctrines of the early Church.

Consider most of the things you know today about Christ and the Church. If there were no doctrines, how would you articulate your belief in the Trinity, Christ as Lord, the Eucharist, marriage, morality, and so on? We read from Saint Paul that all Scripture is useful for teaching (*didache*, doctrine), rebuking, correcting, and training in righteousness (2 Timothy 3:16).

Teaching is an essential aspect of our faith. And teachings, for the most part, are expressed in doctrinal terms. Theology gives us the language as well as ways to articulate these teachings and adapt them to different settings. Dogmas are the core beliefs that are taught. You see how these three go together.

Imagine a church without doctrine. Imagine a faith without condensed codes of belief. Such would be a world without order and faith without direction. Such would be like an information technology web without mark-up languages. Such is a recipe for communicative futility.

REFLECT

In what ways do I promote the authentic doctrine of the Church in my life? To what extent do I know the fundamental tenets of my faith, and how ready am I to share them with joy when I have the opportunity?

PRAY

My Lord and God, the truth and life, continue to guide me as I allow the gospel's truth and sound doctrine to shape my faith life. Amen.

Saturday

Practical Judgment

Readings: Acts 16:1–10; John 15:18–21

In the previous three reflections, I shared some lessons from the First Christian Council in Jerusalem. You may want to refer back to those reflections, but here is a summary: Paul and Barnabas take matters to the Church in Jerusalem to resolve the controversy between themselves and some Jewish Christian converts. The main issue is whether gentiles need to be circumcised in order to be saved. The apostles and presbyters decide that salvation is by God's grace and that circumcision isn't necessary. This decision supports Saint Paul's position.

Nevertheless, we see Paul do something that seems contradictory in his second missionary journey. You may recall that Paul goes on three missionary journeys. The first is to Cyprus and Galatia (see Acts 13:1–14:28). The second is to Europe (see Acts 15:3b–18: 22). The third is to Asia Minor and Europe (see Acts 18:23–21:16).

What Paul does that seems contradictory to his position during the Jerusalem Council of AD 50 is to circumcise Timothy, whose mom is a Jew and whose dad is Greek. Timothy, who is probably a teen or young adult, must have received the gift of faith through his mother. He is well loved and praised by the people of Lystra and Iconium. Paul takes him as a spiritual son and companion working alongside Silas.

Paul's second missionary journey takes him to areas that are predominantly Jewish. Remember, Timothy is a Jew, having been born to a Jewish mom. Paul is concerned that some will object to having Timothy minister to them if he isn't circumcised. Paul fears this will reflect negatively on Timothy and cast a shadow of doubt about his respect for Jewish customs and the Law of Moses. Not being circumcised might call his integrity into question and, I suggest, be bad PR for the ministry in that territory.

To avoid this problem, Paul applies an ethical principle known as practical judgment. He also uses common sense and a touch of PR savvy. Paul knows the right thing. He does the right thing at the right time and for the right reasons. He is prudent. The decision at the Council of Jerusalem isn't intended to destroy the culture of the Jews. Instead, it is intended to save the gentiles from physical circumcision, which has nothing to do with their incorporation as believers in the Lord Jesus Christ.

Nonetheless, to avoid creating an image problem, a stumbling block to their ministry, Paul supports Timothy's circumcision. Perhaps his motivation is to remove any barriers to the more important work of God. Nothing is worth impeding the Good News of Christ. Paul's tactic is worth emulating by evangelizers today.

Consider that in another instance, Paul refuses circumcision for another of his sons, Titus. I suggest it is because Titus is not a Jew but a gentile (see Acts 15:1ff and Galatians 2:3–50). Hence, Paul is not demonstrating a double standard. He is being prudent and applying the same principle of practical judgment.

I'll bet that some Christians today, especially those who act in an ethnocentric manner, would oppose Saint Paul. They might accuse him of being a hypocrite, duplicitous, and a terrible bishop. But truth vindicates itself.

We learn from this situation how to apply a general principle to practical matters. First, we must know precisely what the letters of the Law are and what they mean. Second, we must understand the spirit of the Law. Third, we must apply the Law to concrete situations. As Saint Thomas Aquinas suggests, laws that are not practical are as good as dead.

REFLECT

As a believer, how do I apply practical judgment in balancing the demands of the Law and the spirit of the Law? In what ways do I use the general principles of my faith in situations that yield an ethical dilemma?

PRAY

Lord Jesus, give me the grace to know your mind in every law so I may follow not merely the letters but the spirit of the law. Give me proper discernment to do your will in all things. Amen.

WEEK SIX OF EASTER

Sunday, Year A

Another Counselor

Readings: Acts 8:5–8, 14–17; 1 Peter 3:15–18; John 14:15–21

*G*oodbyes are not the sweetest things in life. Consider the farewell to a child going off to college or a spouse heading to the battlefront. If we had the power, we would be with them all the way, making sure everything was all right.

The moment of goodbye comes to the Lord's disciples. It is the final goodbye. They will not see the Lord Jesus face to face, in his physical body, any longer. Neither will they touch him nor smell his divine aroma. He is going back to the Father, yet he will not leave them alone without the support they need. What a loving Savior!

In the events described in John 14:15–21, the Lord does not wish his believers goodbye without a substitute. Instead, he promises and gifts them (and us) "another presence" like himself.

The apostles and disciples had seen and known Jesus Christ as the "Paraclete" and the counselor. 1 John 2:1 describes Jesus Christ as "Paraclete," which means "advocate": "We have an advocate with the Father, Jesus Christ, the righteous." The Letter to the Hebrews reaffirms the same truth that Jesus is the advocate and mediator for us with the Father (see Hebrews 7:25).

In truth, Jesus Christ is our advocate and mediator. But he is physically leaving the apostles, and they are sad and discouraged, just as we are sad and discouraged when Christ seems distant from us. In those moments, our worries consume our thoughts and emotions. Who will defend us before the world that is opposed to our beliefs and lifestyle? Who will console us? Who will speak on our behalf amidst our powerful adversaries? Who will intervene so our needs are met? Who will accompany us during our moments of sorrow, distress, depression, and anxiety? Who will show us the way? Who will be our companion in moments of loneliness? Who?

Then comes the promise plus the grace from the Lord Jesus Christ himself: "If you love me, you will keep my commandments. And I will pray the Father, and he will give you another Counselor [Paraclete], to be with you forever, even the Spirit of truth, whom the world cannot receive, because it neither sees him nor knows him; you know him, for he dwells with you, and will be in you. I will not leave you desolate; I will come to you" (John 14:15–18).

If you love me, the blessed Lord tells us, keep my commandment. Isn't the most real love experienced when we allow the person we love to influence our decisions? To love someone completely makes us believe without doubt in this person. We rarely find such love in humans. Such love is possible by the grace of love poured into our hearts: "God's love has been poured out into our hearts through the Holy Spirit, who has been given to us" (Romans 5:5).

We see now how this first line (John 14:15) of the Lord's promise connects with the second and subsequent ones: "And I will pray the Father, and he will give you another Counselor to be with you forever . . ."

Please pay attention to the words of Our Savior here. He is not sending us a Paraclete or advocate not related to himself or unlike himself. Instead, he is sending us one who is one with himself.

He is asking the Father, on our behalf, to send us *another* advocate/counselor.

The Lord Jesus is the first advocate, counselor, of the believer. The Holy Spirit is another advocate. The same grace flowing from Jesus flows from "another Counselor," the Holy Spirit, since both of them with the Father are (is) one God. So although Jesus has left the Church (us) physically, he is still fully with us in a unique way through the Holy Spirit.

For the Church today—and this applies to Church members too—this means God continues to be with us in an intimate way just as Jesus came to show us the way to the Trinity. Sound evidence of this presence is the *sensus fidei/sensus fidelium*, that is, the faithful's sense of faith. The Spirit speaks in the faithful through the ages. The Church teaches this truth. Other truths are the sacraments and the Word through which God's life is poured and animated in us by the Spirit. God abides with us, not in physical form as when the Lord Jesus walked the Earth, but through another way, another abiding presence, the Holy Spirit: "I am with you always, to the close of the age" (Matthew 28:20).

There are tons of examples of the fruits of this abiding divine presence of Jesus and the Holy Spirit. The fruitfulness of Philip's ministry and the coming of the same Holy Spirit upon the Samarians in Acts 8 at the behest of Peter and John are good examples. So are other examples in Scripture and the daily life of the Church today. Fruits of evangelization, in which lives are transformed and renewed, are evidence too. God works wonders among the faithful.

The Church today carries in no diminished way the same experiences of the eyewitnesses of Jesus more than two thousand years ago. We are his body. We are his hands. Christ still speaks today. He heals. He counsels. He breaks the shackles of bondage. He is still alive in his body, the Church, through the abiding self of the Holy Spirit, another advocate.

In the reflection of Monday of the sixth week of Easter, I will continue this reflection on the qualities of the Holy Spirit as the Paraclete. Subsequently, I will hint at why the Holy Spirit is called the Spirit of Truth. There will be other truths concerning the Holy Spirit that I will reflect upon as we prepare for the novena (the nine days of prayers) to the Holy Spirit. The novena begins on the evening of Ascension Thursday. Read on!

REFLECT
How am I aware of the abiding presence of the Lord through his Spirit in my life? How can I appreciate the Holy Spirit and be open to him?

PRAY
Oh, Holy Spirit, renew me, revive my weak spirit. Amen.

Sunday, Year B

Friends of God

Readings: Acts 10:25–26, 34–35, 44–48; 1 John 4:7–10;
John 15:9–17

*A*s I read the Gospel of John 15:9–17, a particular line grips me
with renewed interest: the Lord Jesus says, "You are my friends if you
do what I command you. No longer do I call you servants, for the
servant does not know what his master is doing; but I have called you
friends, for all that I have heard from my Father I have made known to
you. You did not choose me, but I chose you and appointed you that
you should go and bear fruit and that your fruit should abide; so that
whatever you ask the Father in my name, he may give it to you. This I
command you, to love one another" (John 15:14–17).

I go back and forth to the line that says, "You are my friends."
First addressed to the apostles, these words are personal to me and I
believe to any believer in the Lord. I feel a deep joy and a profound
peace that the Lord calls me a friend. I also feel unworthy to be among
those who share in this intimate friendship with Christ as a member
of his body, the Church.

Indeed, "friend" here does not mean we are equals with Christ. Saint
Augustine would rather say this word shows how much Christ humbles
himself (condescends) to our level. Christ grants us access to his life. He
does so not only in becoming like us in all things except sin but equally
in the relational example of tender affection and love throughout his
earthly life. He seals his friendship with the greatest love—dying on the
cross—so that, in him, we find the fullness of life and glory.

Christ chooses us to be his friends. We don't choose him to be our friend (John 15:16). This truth, to me, is strikingly beautiful. Not only has he chosen us to be his friends but he also gives us the inner power, the grace, to make this friendship come alive, mature, and produce much fruit. The fruit isn't fruit such as the termite-infested nuts on a barren farm in southern California or the mangled, pale-looking oranges hanging off the drought-stricken trees during harsh weather in the Savannahs. Rather, this fruit is healthy, delicious, and everlasting, with the glowing foliage of health.

Saint Paul calls such fruits "fruits of righteousness" (Philippians 1:11). This means holiness of life, a life that is justified, a life that glorifies God. In such life, we see personal virtues such as those listed in Galatians 5:22 and called the fruits of the Spirit, namely love, joy, peace, patience, kindness, goodness, faithfulness, gentleness, and self-control.

We also produce fruits of evangelization. That is, through our witness, many will come to glorify God (Matthew 5:16) and come to life in Christ. A fruitful friend of Jesus wins more friends for Christ. It is a normal consequence of that friendship. We read about Saint Peter in Acts 10, living that fruitful life of friendship with Christ. The spirit of Christ, the Holy Spirit, is at work among peoples, showing that the fruit is not limited to a particular race. Saint Peter and all who have become friends of Christ from the early Church to our current era bear fruits of evangelization. I hope you and I bear fruit too.

How can this be when we are simply human? How can we truly abide in Christ and produce much fruit when, in ourselves, we often falter? Christ himself gives us the answer. First, we strive not to lose sight of our source or disconnect with our source, where we belong, to whom we have been reborn. We cannot grow and produce fruit on our own. In matters of spiritual growth and fruitfulness, the notion of "self-made man" is an empty claim. It's preposterous. We grow if we depend on the grace of God.

Second, friendship with God also implies friendship within his body. We produce fruits when we are grafted in the body of Christ. Abiding in him is regularly abiding in his body. He has nobody else on Earth today except the Church where, through those graces he has promised, he nourishes and strengthens the bond of love he has established with us. Though friendship with God is a personal relationship, it is also a relationship within his community of faith, the Church.

Third, the power of this relationship does not come from us. It comes from Christ himself. He gives it when he sends the Holy Spirit. It is the Holy Spirit, what Saint Paul describes as "God's love poured into our heart through the Holy Spirit given to us" (Romans 5:5), that makes us truly reciprocal friends of God. This Spirit is the abiding grace of Christ for us, within our hearts. The Spirit stirs us and inspires us to do good, produce beautiful fruits, and sometimes perform miracles. The same Spirit at work in the early Church is at work today in the Church and the hearts and minds of God's present-day friends.

Fourth, this friendship with Christ, which comes to us through the light of faith, is lived or expressed in the works of charity (Galatians 5:6). The Lord says to us, those called his friends, "You are my friends if you do what I command you" (John 15:14). He says it differently earlier: "If you keep my commandments, you will abide in my love . . ." (John 15:10).

Friendship with God isn't, therefore, only about a feeling of friendship or a mental state where we live in the euphoria of love without action. Instead, there is an expectation from our side regarding what we can give back. It is what indeed proves the depth of our love.

Though this reciprocal love is mild and imperfect compared to God's love, it is acceptable because the love of God himself inspires it. This is what keeping Christ's commandment is—love. It is the kind that is ready to offer back to the friend we have in Jesus what we have become. It is the type that relates to any person despite where they come from and their situation in life with selflessness, following in the footsteps of Christ.

Love without boundaries. Love in Christ. This is the way to true friendship with him who has loved us first. What a beautiful thing to know and remind ourselves of this sixth Sunday of the Resurrection!

REFLECT
How do I feel knowing that God has granted me the privilege to call him friend? How can I show gratitude for this great treasure of friendship with God?

PRAY
I pray that the Spirit of God, God's love, will be poured into my heart and the hearts of others. May my life express gratitude to the Lord for the grace of divine friendship. Amen.

Sunday, Year C

God's Abiding Presence

Readings: Acts 15:1–2, 22–29; Revelation 21:10–14, 22–23; John 14:23–29

We have been journeying with the early Church through the forty days of Easter and are approaching the last week of the season. We have seen how the Church lives and shares the life of the Resurrection. Since the Feast of Ascension, which marks the beginning of the Pentecost novena, takes place on Thursday this week, I will gradually introduce a core subject in our spiritual lives. It is the theme of the Third Person of the blessed Trinity, the Holy Spirit.

The first recorded polarizing conflict in the early Church happened at Antioch. As we saw earlier, some excessively enthusiastic Jewish converts to Christianity preached and demanded that the gentiles be circumcised and follow the Mosaic Law to be saved. Paul and Barnabas and a few other leaders of the Church in Antioch opposed this heresy. The groups brought the matter to Jerusalem to the First Christian Council (or Jerusalem Council) in AD 50 for apostolic resolution.

The council decided that gentiles don't need circumcision to be saved, that God's grace saves them through faith in Jesus (see Acts 15:1ff). Here, I want to focus on the authority referenced by the apostles as evidence of their decision. Here is the text: "It has seemed good to the Holy Spirit and to us to lay upon you no greater burden than these necessary things . . ." (Acts 15:28). You see that the apostles appeal to two authorities: the Holy Spirit and "us."

This line of Scripture is powerful. In addition to acknowledging the Holy Spirit's ever-abiding presence in the life of the Church, it reveals the unique role of the apostles of Jesus in the revelatory work of God in Christ. Their position is unique. Their bridging role of connecting the Old Testament with the reality of the Christ event is indispensable. The "us" is striking because it is an appeal to this indispensable place of apostolic abstraction and transmission of divine revelation.

In the book of Revelation, John's vision at the Island of Patmos is a confirmation of the foundation of the Church, built on twelve pillars—the Twelve Apostles—and also appealing to the imagery of the twelve tribes of Israel, which in turn connects the promise made to Abraham to the new covenant fulfillment in Christ. Thus there are many significant points encapsulated in John's vision.

How is this ongoing revelatory communication between the Old Testament and the New Testament possible after Jesus is gone? The Lord gives the picture, or should I say the answer. First, he promises that if we listen to him and keep his commandment, he and God the Father will abide with us, that is, make a home in us (see John 14:23). This abiding is possible through the love between the Father and the Son—the Holy Spirit.

See an example (there are numerous) of the fulfillment of this promise. The first ecclesial but also theological crisis in the Church (see Acts 15:1–25) is resolved by the counseling, teaching, and remembering roles of the Holy Spirit. The Spirit is with the disciples during the entire debate of the Jerusalem Council. The apostles themselves profess that the Holy Spirit is with them as they make their decisions. They don't resolve the doctrinal issues by their own mere human opinions. They collaborate with the Holy Spirit: "the Holy Spirit and us . . ." (Acts 15:28).

This is a crucial lesson for us in our different leadership roles in our parishes and domestic churches (the family). During administrative decisions or theological debates, do we allow the Holy Spirit to teach us and inspire us? When conflicts arise in the family, do we listen and hear what the Spirit of God has to say? How often do we make the Holy Spirit the soul of our decision-making process?

If you wish to discern correctly, give the Holy Spirit a chance.

REFLECT

What in my life and way of doing things is a barrier to the Holy Spirit's works? What am I going to do to allow the Spirit to be central in my life?

PRAY

Lord, I surrender to you. I open my heart to your Spirit. Holy Spirit, take charge and lead me to what you want, where you want it, and how you want it. Amen.

Alternative Reflection

Led by the Holy Spirit

Readings: Acts 15:1–2, 22–29; Revelation 21:10–14, 22–23; John 14:23–29

I draw from Acts of the Apostles, chapter 15, and the Gospel of John, chapter 14:23–29, to highlight a couple of roles the Holy Spirit plays in the Church and in the lives of believers.

The Lord Jesus Christ promises us that if we listen to him and keep his commandments, he and God the Father will abide with us.

That is, God will make a home in us (see John 14:23). This abiding presence comes through the love from the Father and the Son—the Holy Spirit. God's love has been poured into the hearts of believers through the Holy Spirit (see Romans 5:5).

The Lord makes us this promise, and his word is true: "These things I have spoken to you while I am still with you. But the Counselor, the Holy Spirit, whom the Father will send in my name, he will teach you all things, and bring to your remembrance all that I have said to you" (John 14:25–26).

Observe the two functions the Holy Spirit will carry out in the life of the Church based on the revelation of this particular text. First, the Holy Spirit will teach you all things. The Holy Spirit will teach the Church and believers all things about the salvation Christ has brought. The Spirit will make the gospel come alive in the Church. Anyone led by the Holy Spirit begins to see the richness of divine revelation in Christ, not only in the written text of Scripture and sacred worship but also in everyday life.

Second, the Holy Spirit will make believers remember what has been revealed in the Old Testament. The Holy Spirit will make believers understand the things Jesus Christ has said and done and all he has taught the disciples, which seems way over their heads. The Holy Spirit reminds the Church and believers of Jesus' events. Wow!

Hence, the Holy Spirit is called "Counselor" for the roles of teaching and reminding. The Spirit is called "Comforter" for the role of consoling us with peace and confidence of being right with God. Christ's promise to be with the Church until the end of time (see Matthew 28:20) is, therefore, possible through the Holy Spirit. He is God's abiding presence with us.

You have to be confident of this: with the Holy Spirit, an unnerving case becomes a smoother ride. One thing is needed: let us allow the Holy Spirit to direct the Church. Let us give the Spirit a chance in our families. If the Spirit abides with us, we are better for it.

REFLECT

How open am I to the teaching role of the Holy Spirit? When I read Scripture, for instance, do I seek the Spirit's guidance to help me know and remember God's Word?

PRAY

Come, Holy Spirit, fill the hearts of the faithful and kindle in us the fire of your love. Enlighten my mind to your teaching and make me remember as the Lord continues to speak through his body. Amen.

Monday

The Holy Spirit As Our Advocate

Readings: Acts 16:11–15; John 15:26–16:4a

*P*reviously, I introduced the theme of the Holy Spirit. This reflection on the Holy Spirit's attribute as the Paraclete, the gift of God the Son from the Father, flows from the preceding line of thought.

In continuation of the farewell address to his disciples and the promise of another advocate, the Lord Jesus says this: "But when the Counselor (παράκλητος) comes, whom I shall send to you from the Father, even the Spirit of truth, who proceeds from the Father, he will bear witness to me; and you also are witnesses, because you have been with me from the beginning" (John 15:26–27).

The Greek word παράκλητος (*parakletos*), sometimes anglicized as "Paraclete," has rich meaning. It encompasses some crucial qualities we should know about the Holy Spirit and his work in the believer's and the Church's life. Observe that I always mention the Holy Spirit's work in the Church as well as in individual members of the Church. This is because the gift of the Holy Spirit is for us as the Church and as individuals in the Church.

During his opening address at the third session of Vatican II on September 14, 1964, Pope Paul VI insisted we pay attention to these two areas of the Spirit's work: "The Holy Spirit acts internally within each person, as well as on the whole community [the Church], animating, vivifying, sanctifying."

From his commentary on the Gospel of John, seventeenth-century Flemish Jesuit Bible scholar Cornelius à Lapide offers a systematized classification of the meaning of *parakletos*. According to him, it includes an advocate or intercessor, an exhorter or inciter, and a comforter.[11]

Consider the many times we need someone called in to provide a helping hand to our "helpless" or challenging situation. There are many things about us—weak and imperfect as we are—that make us get on our knees or crawl into bed, unwilling to leave our room. We feel deeply in need. Moments like these, and many more in our spiritual lives, compel Jesus the Lord to *call in* the person of the Divine Spirit, the Holy Spirit, to help our needy situation.

The word "Paraclete," as you may know, literally means "someone called in." The person is called in to supply our need or be an advocate to our cause. The Spirit comes in to refresh, revitalize, and renew our depressed spirit.

The Holy Spirit supplies the needs of the Church and the believer through at least three distinct ways. First is by being our holy and

---

11.   Cornelius à Lapide, *The Great Commentary of Cornelius À Lapide: S. John's Gospel—Chaps. 12 to 21 and Epistles 1, 2, and 3*, trans. Thomas W. Mossman, Fourth Edition., vol. 6 (Edinburgh: John Grant, 1908), p. 145.

loving advocate. The Holy Spirit carries on in the Church and in us the same intercessory role of Christ the Lord. The Spirit becomes our voice in prayer, offering our needs and sacrifices in his voice to God the Father and the Son. Our public prayer (Sacred Liturgy) is alive and effective because of the Holy Spirit.

Romans 8:26 reassures us of this intercessory role of the Holy Spirit: "Likewise, the Spirit helps us in our weakness; for we do not know how to pray as we ought, but the Spirit himself intercedes for us with sighs too deep for words." God understands that conversation because it is of his Spirit.

In our prayers, even those imperfect conversations with God, if we allow the Holy Spirit to do so, he will plead our cause before God. He will speak perfectly on our behalf. He does so because he is our advocate, the promise by Christ the Incarnate Advocate to us as believers.

So when the Church prays during the liturgy or when individuals pray in private or public, those prayers resound in the throne of Divine Love. They echo the power and voice of the Spirit of God within us. Our private prayers are as good as our openness to the anointing of the Holy Spirit.

REFLECT

How do I appreciate the role of the Holy Spirit as my advocate? Can I think of an example of when the Holy Spirit stirred my heart and inspired me with answers when I needed them the most? Am I willing to share my testimony with others as a way of encouragement in their situation?

PRAY

O Holy Spirit, thank you for being my advocate. Amen.

Tuesday

The Holy Spirit As Our Counselor and Exhorter

Readings: Acts 16:22–34; John 16:5–11

I continue our reflection on the Holy Spirit, the Paraclete. Here, I look at how the Holy Spirit is our counselor and exhorter.

Perhaps you became aware of the vital role of a counselor when you were in high school or college. Counselors help us to make the right choices in our career paths.

The words "I will go see my counselor" seem to suggest a belief that the counselor will figure things out or at least help us to do so. We realize that the counselor's job is relevant because we are at crossroads or discerning a situation or a thing. Counselors can also help us find the right mental or emotional disposition or sense of balance towards a particular or many situations.

Whether the counselor offers clinical, spiritual, or educational services, he or she is "called in" as a second expert voice. In a similar but most profound way, the Holy Spirit is the counselor graciously offered to us from the Father through Jesus Christ the Son. The Lord Jesus tells the disciples, "Nevertheless I tell you the truth: it is to your advantage that I go away, for if I do not go away, the Counselor will not come to you; but if I go, I will send him to you" (John 16:7).

Making the right decisions regarding our lives and futures as well as discerning the right spiritual path in our relationship with God and one another isn't easy. Hence, the Holy Spirit helps us, guiding and urging us to make the right choices.

If you find it challenging to maintain a consistent pattern of good behavior or make the right choices, you have no better answer than the Holy Spirit. If you feel like making progress in the invitation to be holy is frustrating, call in the Holy Spirit. He will counsel and advise you. This solution applies to the individual as well as the Church as a community of faith. Pastors in parishes, leaders of ministries, parents in families, and teachers in schools need the Holy Spirit's counsel to lead well.

One has to praise God for the mighty works done in the early Church and the Church today, such as the miracle the Spirit provides for Paul and Silas. Their courage while in prison and how they boldly keep faith in the risen Lord (Acts 16:22–34) are testimonials of the great power of the Spirit influencing their lives.

The counseling work of the Holy Spirit also keeps us genuinely attuned to the will of God. Often, we ignore or explain away the weight of sin or lack of love and ignore the good. The Holy Spirit, as our counselor, is the source of moral and spiritual clarity. The Spirit shines the light of truth in our lives and hearts so we see the good as it truly is and evil as terrible as it is.

As the Lord Jesus says, "And when he [Holy Spirit] comes, he will convince the world concerning sin and righteousness and judgment: concerning sin, because they do not believe in me; concerning righteousness, because I go to the Father, and you will see me no more; concerning judgment because the ruler of this world is judged" (John 16:8–11).

> ### REFLECT
> When I am stuck, am I aware that the Holy Spirit is ever present to help me resolve the challenges I face? Do I trust the Spirit to spur me to the right direction and help me in my dilemma?

> **PRAY**
> O Holy Spirit, be my counselor as I rise in the morning and go back to bed at night. Amen.

Wednesday

Walk and Run

Readings: Acts 17:15, 22–18:1; John 16:12–15

*T*he ancient Greeks were remarkable in their search for knowledge. Centuries before the modern mind could pride itself on liberal thoughts and beliefs, knowledge was already part of their culture. Athens was the hub of that culture, and Areopagus was the stage upon which the best of innovative human ideas rallied in Athens.

The Athenians cherished freedom of expression and, in particular, freedom of speech. This freedom was granted to all, both babblers and the articulate. No one was silenced in the public forum, not even one with news as strange as the Resurrection. Anyone with something to say, especially what had not been heard before, had the full attention of the curious Greeks.

Saint Paul found himself in Athens on the hill, Areopagus, where Socrates, Plato, Aristotle, and other great Greek philosophers had shared their ideas. He was brought to the stage by others who heard him speak about "some deity." As some of them said, "He seems to be a preacher of foreign divinities" (see Acts 17:18).

From Paul, we learn how to engage a people's culture. Paul begins by acknowledging the religious sentiments of the native people: "I see you are very religious." Starting with what is good in a people's culture or worldview is always an excellent strategy to adopt if an evangelizer wants to engage other cultures, traditions, and faith claims.

For the best of Greek minds, belief in the supernatural was natural. Their quest for more meaning in religion was not about whether God exists but what type of God exists. Since they weren't sure, their accommodating spirit made space for even an "unknown god."

They gave room to accommodate their limitations. They didn't want to miss anything. Observe that it was all about them searching for God. Paul comes with totally different news, and evangelizers should pay attention to it. One of the radical things about Christianity is that it is not about humanity's search for God. Rather, it is about God's search for us. From the call of Abraham through the prophets and the fullest of revelation in Christ, it is about God drawing us to himself.

This news was different, as was the news about the resurrection of Jesus from the dead. The latter, the Athenians could not grasp at all. Hence, they invite Paul to come next time if he wishes them to hear him again (Acts 17:32).

Further lessons for Christian evangelization: remaining at the level of what is common to the people (an understanding of God that doesn't draw us to the deeper reality of God's revelation of himself) isn't the wisest tactic. It is spiritually crippling. To walk and run, to grow into spiritual maturity, we need to learn that faith is the belief in what God does and is doing for us, not what we are doing for God. It is our being part of God's plan even if it is mind blowing, as the Resurrection was to the Athenians.

I will show you, starting tomorrow, who it is that makes the faith come alive. To preempt myself, it is the Holy Spirit.

REFLECT

As I grow in my knowledge of the Lord, how does it influence how I do things in society? How does the Spirit lead me in navigating the complex world around me?

PRAY

Lord Jesus Christ, give me the grace to appreciate your love for me so I can have a more intimate relationship with you. Amen.

Thursday

The Ascension of the Lord— Hope and Commission

Readings, Year A: Acts 1:1–11; Ephesians 1:17–23; Matthew 28:16–20

Reading, Year B: Mark 16:15–20

Alternative Readings, Year B: Ephesians 4:1–13 or Ephesians 4:1–7, 11–13

Reading, Year C: Luke 24:46–53

Alternative Readings, Year C: Hebrew 9:24–28; 10:19–23

*R*eflect on two unique moments when the Lord Jesus offers farewell words to his disciples. The first is on the eve of his arrest during the Last Supper. During the supper, he leaves instructions to his apostles:

"Do this in memory of me." These are the words of the institution of the Eucharist. Following this is the Lord's moving action of washing the feet of the disciples and asking them to do the same. In our faith tradition, we see this latter act as part of the institution of church leadership—the sacrament of holy orders.

This goodbye is not the Lord's final goodbye to his disciples. The second and final goodbye of Jesus in bodily form occurs at the ascension. Scripture records the moving scene: "But you shall receive power when the Holy Spirit has come upon you, and you shall be my witnesses . . . And when he had said this, as they were looking on, he was lifted up, and a cloud took him out of their sight. And while they were gazing into heaven as he went, behold, two men stood by them in white robes, and said, 'Men of Galilee, why do you stand looking into heaven? This Jesus, who was taken up from you into heaven, will come in the same way as you saw him go into heaven'" (Acts 1:8–11).

No, these verses don't seem like a hallucination as some critiques who deny the Ascension argue. Not all of the apostles would be hallucinating at the same time. Moreover, the use of vivid phrases like, "as they were living," "a cloud took him," and "while they were still gazing" are testimonies of firsthand witnesses. Besides, there is a clear message from two angels testifying the truth as to the reality of the Ascension.

The point is this: this final goodbye from the Lord Jesus is dramatic. Perhaps the Lord wants the memory to stick. This ascension message is consistent in all three synoptic gospels (Matthew, Mark, and Luke). Namely, you will receive the Holy Spirit so you can bear witness to these.

If you relate this final goodbye to the Last Supper goodbye, you have the complete picture of the Lord Jesus' will. It's as though he is saying to his followers, I am done with my mission on Earth. Now is your time to continue it to the ends of the Earth. You do so by celebrating me in the Eucharist and bearing witness to me with your life, such as leading by example of service and letting others know what I have done. All this is possible by the Holy Spirit I will send you so you can bear witness.

The event and message of Ascension emphasize four truths to me, and they are worth pondering and acting upon:

The Great Commission to evangelize is a primary task of every believer.

The Great Commission to evangelize is rooted in the Eucharist.

The Eucharist is brought about through the sacrament of service in the Church called the holy orders.

All the other sacraments prepare us not only to grow in Christ but to draw others to Christ.

Evangelization is, therefore, a central mission of the Church. A failure to evangelize is a failure in our mission as the Church. But evangelization is only possible through the power of the Holy Spirit, God's gift to us, through Jesus Christ the Lord.

REFLECT

What do I learn from the message of the ascension of the Lord? In what ways may I live out the Great Commission, love for the Eucharist, and service?

PRAY

Lord Jesus, keep the memory of your will in my mind and heart so I can always boldly tell the story of my redemption in you. Amen.

Alternative Reflection

Wait and Receive

Readings, Year A: Acts 1:1–11; Ephesians 1:17–23;
Matthew 28:16–20

Reading, Year B: Mark 16:15–20

Alternative Readings, Year B: Ephesians 4:1–13
or Ephesians 4:1–7, 11–13

Reading, Year C: Luke 24:46–53

Alternative Readings, Year C: Hebrew 9:24–28; 10:19–23

I share the need to wait to receive the grace to lead God's way. I draw inspiration from the last words of the Lord Jesus Christ as he ascends to heaven (Luke 24:50–53).

The Gospel of Luke reports, "Then he led them [the disciples] out as far as Bethany and lifting up his hands he blessed them. While he blessed them, he parted from them and was carried up into heaven. And they worshipped him, and returned to Jerusalem with great joy, and were continually in the temple blessing God" (Luke 24:50–53).

The Lord never ceases blessing us. When he calls, he blesses. When he commissions us to do something, he blesses us with the grace to perform those roles effectively.

As the Lord blesses us, he also asks us to wait on him all the way. We don't run faster than the Lord. We don't assume it is our doing. We don't want to lead the Lord. We want the Lord to lead us.

With the Lord's calling, there is a constant appeal to trust in providence. This trust holds us back from excessive zeal or impatience because we want to see an immediate outcome. I know we want to see results right away, but the Lord's path isn't simply about results. It is about fidelity. As one of the famous lines of Saint Teresa Calcutta, Mother Teresa, suggests, it isn't "about your success but your faithfulness."

We could learn from the early disciples how to respond when the Lord tells us to wait. Their response was worship. Their hearts were full of joy. The blessings of God and our response in prayer fill us with immeasurable joy.

To wait is to live the life of worship. We don't wait aimlessly, nor do we allow our minds to be preoccupied with empty and vain thoughts. We wait in worship.

In worship, we wait on the Lord, and we revere his complex plans and providence. In worship, we allow ourselves to be drawn into the divine way of being. We live in the now of divine providence. This is why, many times in worship, we lose a sense of time, having been drawn into timelessness in a brief moment. To wait on the Lord is to be at his service in worship. It is to trust in divine providence.

We wait to see, to encounter glory. We wait for the fulfillment of the promise and the maturation of the blessing the Lord has given.

In a nutshell, this waiting is the story of the Christian spiritual life. Our blessings don't take on a mere icing-on-the-cake experience. Our blessings mature and produce much joy as we wait on the Lord. They flourish as we do, which is precisely what the Lord asks. They blossom as we respond in worship.

In our blessings are what we have received and what is yet to come. The Lord does not give us mere perishable things. Whatever the Lord gives us—shelter, food, friends, family, and so on— are all geared toward the glory to come. In divine blessing is provident hope.

We wait with the blessings we have received in the promise of many more blessings to come.

Ascension feast is a celebration of this hope in Christ. Henceforth, we wait. We wait for the promise of the Holy Spirit. The Spirit descends into the waiting heart, the heart attuned to worship. We who have received the Spirit wait in anticipation of many more of this Spirit's graces as we experience the fullness of glory to come.

Therefore, we wait in hope in Christ. This hope does not fail us (see Romans 5:5). We know for sure that the Lord whom we love and worship ascended so we can be welcomed in the Father's home. We wait. We worship.

REFLECT
How often do I wait on the Lord? Do I get ahead of God because I want things my way?

PRAY
I pray for the grace of dynamic faith and living hope. Amen.

Friday

On the Traditional Gifts of the Holy Spirit—
Pentecost Novena, Day One

Readings: Acts 18:9–18; John 16:20–23

I welcome you to day one of the novena to the Holy Spirit. Did you know that this is the novena of all novenas? You are probably familiar with different novenas in our Catholic Christian spirituality—Marian novenas, the novena to Saint Joseph, the novena to Saint Jude, the novena to Saint Theresa, and so on, but did you know that all these novenas emanate from the first novena ever in the history of the Church? This is the novena to the Holy Spirit.

This is the novena right from the mouth of the Lord Jesus as he is ascending to his Father. He tells the disciples to stay in Jerusalem and be baptized with the Holy Spirit (see Acts 1:4–5).

The disciples don't know what that means or how long they are to wait. Thank God, they obey the Lord and remain in prayer. Providentially, the Holy Spirit comes on the ninth day. Thus we have the name "novena," which is Latin for nine.

The practice of saying novena prayers in anticipation of the Holy Spirit's coming upon the Church was lost for centuries. It pleased the Lord to restore it in 1897, when Pope Leo XIII issued an encyclical titled *Divinum Illud Munus* (*On the Holy Spirit*). In that encyclical, the Holy Father called for a novena (nine days of prayer to the Holy Spirit) throughout the Church in anticipation of Pentecost day.

What might our objective be for these nine days of prayer to the Holy Spirit? Our reflection style should change to a devotional to connect us with the coming of the Holy Spirit. May we reflect on what the first disciples did in anticipation of the promised gift. They obeyed the Lord Jesus, went back to Jerusalem, and started to pray.

On this first day of our novena, let us open our hearts to hear Jesus speak to us, listening to him as he says, "My child, I want to give you the special gift. The gift of my Spirit, the advocate."

If you have received the sacrament of confirmation, you have received the Holy Spirit. The Lord wants a revitalized presence of his Spirit, too, which the Church invites us to welcome. If you have not received the sacrament of confirmation, the novena to the Holy Spirit is even more appropriate for you.

The novena renews our Spirit, making our hearts more docile to the Holy Spirit within us. For those who have not received him the first time, the novena makes them more disposed to the Holy Spirit's renewal.

I ask that you have some quiet time this evening or at your convenience to pray the classic prayer to the Holy Spirit called "Veni Creator Spiritus." You may find this prayer in the appendix on the last pages of this book. Meditate on these words and pray over them as you meditate on Acts. 1:1–5.

REFLECT

Am I ready to open my heart to the anointing power of the Holy Spirit? Do I entertain doubts concerning the incredible works of the Holy Spirit or suppose it is not meant for me? Do I really know about the role of the Holy Spirit in my life as a believer?

> **PRAY**
> Come, Holy Spirit, fill the hearts of the faithful; enkindle in them the fire of your love. Dispose me to welcome you in my heart too. Amen.

Saturday

On the Traditional Gifts of the Holy Spirit— Pentecost Novena, Day Two

Readings: Acts 18: 23–28; John 16:23b–28

I welcome you to day two of our Pentecost novena. I hope you spent some time dusting your heart of some of those worries that distract you from focusing on this special gift of God to us—the Holy Spirit.

Yesterday, we learned how to be open to Jesus Christ. Simply trust him. He is the giver of the gifts. He is not going to force us. He needs us to generously open our hearts so the fountain of his generosity, his promised gift, the Holy Spirit, will fill our thirsty souls.

Consider who the Holy Spirit is and what the gift means for us. In the prophecy of Isaiah 11:1–3, we hear of the seven traditional gifts of the Holy Spirit: wisdom, knowledge, understanding, counsel, fortitude, piety, and awe of the Lord.

If you meditated on the poem "Veni Creator Spiritus" that I recommended yesterday (and every day as this novena evolves), you asked for these gifts. These gifts mean so much in our spiritual lives, and desiring them is the way to go during this novena. We pray today specifically for knowledge as we continue the novena prayer, "Veni Creator Spiritus," in the appendix.

REFLECT

O Holy Spirit! A friend like no one else, the counselor and the consoler, I turn to you because I acknowledge I don't know much. Yes, I have read a lot about you, the Father, and the Son. I have been through many religious formation classes to know more about God and deepen my faith, yet I still don't seem to connect the dots. You are more profound than anything I can fully understand. Nevertheless, you alone can satisfy my yearnings.

I feel that my brain, mind, and intellect are like a filter. I get excited at some information and then, a few steps away, they seem gone like the wind. I need to be equipped with the gift of knowledge. I believe you want me to know. Such knowledge will help me make informed decisions and choices for your glory and the service of my neighbors.

O Holy Spirit! This knowledge of yours, from you and for you, will help me too in my life in society as I shine the light for everyone to see.

PRAY

Come, Holy Spirit. Fill my heart with the knowledge of you, the Father and the Spirit. Let me know as I am known. Amen.

WEEK SEVEN OF EASTER

Seventh Sunday of Easter

They Devoted Themselves to Prayer

Readings, Year A: Acts 1:12–14; 1 Peter 4:13–16; John 17:1–14a

Readings, Year B: Acts 1:15–17, 20a, 20c–26; 1 John 4:11–16; John 17:11b–19

Readings, Year C: Acts 7:55–60; Revelation 22:12–14, 16–17, 20; John 17:20–26

We have journeyed through six weeks of the Resurrection. During this seventh and last week of Easter, the Church invites us to reflect on and follow in the footsteps of the early Church, the first witnesses of the Resurrection, by keeping a novena. See how Acts of the Apostles 1:14 describes it: "All these with one accord devoted themselves to prayer, together with the women and Mary the Mother of Jesus, and with his brethren."

The right disposition in this last week of the celebration of Easter is to keep a novena. We know "the devout prayer" of the disciples numbering about one hundred and twenty people lasted nine days before the Holy Spirit came on the Pentecost. Hence, we have the name novena prayer.

Mother Mary, the Holy Spirit's spouse, who was with the apostles and disciples during the first Christian novena, will accompany us in our prayer. Journeying with her is the best.

In John 17, the Lord Jesus prays intensely. This prayer is called the "Priestly Prayer of Jesus." Unlike the Lord's Prayer, during which the Lord shows us how to pray, this prayer is the actual dialogue between Jesus and the Father.

According to *The Navarre Bible Commentary on Saint John's Gospel* (2005), the "Priestly Prayer of Jesus" comprises three parts. The first part (verses 1–5) contains Jesus' prayer for "the glorification of his holy human nature and the acceptance, by the Father of his sacrifice on the cross." The second part (verses 6–19) is the Lord's prayer for his disciples, the future witnesses to his glory. The Lord's prayer for the unity of believers is the last part (verses 20–26).

In describing the importance of this prayer of Jesus, Saint Augustine reminds us it is also about the Lord showing us how to pray. Prayer, therefore, is an essential aspect of our spiritual lives. The Church gathered in assembly is the Church united to pray, anointed and inspired by the Holy Spirit.

During the first novena to the Holy Spirit, the early believers were united in prayer. Then the Holy Spirit visited them as a Church. Recall the Lord tells us that where two or three are gathered in his name, he will be there in their midst (see Matthew 18:20).

Our prayers are most effective if we invite the Holy Spirit to accompany us as we pray because he is the one who knows God's mind (see 1 Corinthians 2:11). This Spirit is of unity and peace. His coming is to bring order and peace to humans who are not fully living in the grace of glory. God's glory is manifested when we are "fully living." As Saint Irenacus, one of the foremost theologians of the Church, stated, "*Gloria Dei est vivens homo*" (The Glory of God is a living man).

Please remember to continue the novena prayer, "Veni Creator Spiritus."

REFLECT

Do I know the Holy Spirit? Who is the Holy Spirit to me? Have I welcomed him in my life? In my spiritual life, have I allowed the Holy Spirit to inspire me and teach me how to pray? To what extent have I listened as the Spirit whispers the promptings of a prayerful sentiments?

PRAY

As I continue the novena to the Holy Spirit, I pray that the Holy Spirit, the sanctifier, may fill my heart with the love of the Father and the Son. May he revitalize the graces I have been given so that I will be truly aglow for God. Amen.

Sunday

Pentecost Novena, Day Three

On this third day of the novena to the Holy Spirit, we ask for the grace of understanding.

"Faith seeking understanding" is the famous motto of Saint Anselm. Understanding doesn't come that easily. It doesn't come merely by our handiwork alone but by the Holy Spirit's grace. The Spirit opens our minds, our intellect, so that we can penetrate the revealed truths about God and the things in the world. The gift of understanding makes simple and more apparent, indeed relational, what is complex. Don't we need that gift to better see the path God has set for us in our relationship with him?

Likewise, we need the gift of understanding to make the right decisions, to know what is essential and what isn't. A better understanding of the world and the environment in which we live helps us live peacefully and happily. The gift of understanding also affords us many blessings of emotional intelligence in which we grow in awareness of ourselves, our environment, and the people with whom we relate.

Similarly, the gift of understanding helps us develop healthy relationships with one another, especially those who are difficult. Empathy grows from the gift of understanding too. How much we need this gift today!

Remember to continue the novena prayer, "Veni Creator Spiritus."

REFLECT

As I ask to know you more, Lord Jesus, bless me to understand what I know. I wish to understand things that I should. This understanding will enable me to judge better things, events, news, and the world around me.

O Holy Spirit, many times I read the word of the Son in Scripture and don't seem to understand. I often read holy and spiritual books from your saints and they are over my head. Is it because of my poor education or lack of ability to understand the words? How about gifting me with the same gift you gave to people like Saint John Mary Vianney? He hardly passed his exams, yet you made him understand your word and other people's words in a profound way. He had profound intuition into things.

Holy Spirit, permit me to make one more request. How about blessing me with other gifts too that are connected with the gifts of knowledge and understanding? I mean those charisms that will deepen my knowledge and understanding for better service to your people and the Church. I need your word of knowledge and wisdom and your word of understanding. These serve the needs of my community as well.

I desire that the gifts you give will be for service and not for my self-interest. I believe that when your gifts, Holy Spirit, are used well, they help promote your kingdom on earth. Your name is glorified too. The fruits you give will flourish in my life as well.

PRAY

O Holy Spirit, open my mind to understand your revelations. May I comprehend my place in the plan so I may glorify the Trinity by my words and my deeds. Amen.

Monday

Pentecost Novena, Day Four

Readings for Monday of the Seventh Week of Easter: Acts 19:1–8; John 16:29–33

I welcome you to day four of the novena to the Holy Spirit. On this particular day of grace, let's ask the Lord Jesus Christ to gift us with wisdom.

Remember to continue the novena prayer, "Veni Creator Spiritus."

REFLECT

O Holy Spirit, I know you are the giver of wisdom. I know the Son is Divine Logos, Divine Wisdom, the one who was with the Father even before the world was made (see Proverbs 8:22). I need the gift of wisdom.

I confess that I can't fully comprehend the depth of your revelation. I am working toward it, thanks to your gift of understanding. I need the wisdom to deepen my knowledge and understanding, especially in setting the right priorities.

Our world is becoming more and more complicated. For you, I know it isn't, because with wisdom, nothing is complicated. But for me, there are so many things going on— bills, workload, anxiety, domestic problems, and the fast pace of things, thanks to an instant gratification culture—that sometimes I'm overwhelmed. The mound of information I have to deal with makes life cumbersome. The complicated world of technology, a complex economic system, the weird world of entertainment, and various wants and demands add to the load. All these and more are sometimes overwhelming. I find it challenging to prioritize.

How can I see things in their right perspective without you? From your seat of wisdom, I know things look clear. You know the chaff and the substance and how to separate the two. The opposite is my pitiable state; I don't always discern the difference.

Often, because I do not know the difference, I pursue the shadow. In the end, I waste my precious time on things that are not relevant while skipping relevant things.

I need your wisdom to see things as they should be seen. I need the wisdom to observe things as they should be observed. Wisdom will help me place all the noisy, clashing worldly interests and cares—fame, money, enjoyment, everything—in their right perspective.

It is your wisdom that can reconnect me with the innocence that was destroyed by Original Sin. May I receive that grace of wisdom so that my heart, reconfigured to the Son, Jesus Christ, can see with purity how God sees.

Your wisdom is the power of common sense. Many times I seem not to understand what that means anymore. I need more common sense so that I can make sense of the world around me.

Also, wisdom will help me know the other gifts you have given me and help me understand why and how you want them to be used. I simply want to do your will.

PRAY

With the Church, I pray, "Lord, let your wisdom be with me to help me and to work with me." Amen.

Tuesday

Pentecost Novena, Day Five

Readings: Acts 20:17–27; John 17:1–11a

Did you pray for wisdom yesterday? I prayed for it because I need more of it each day.

On this fifth day of our novena, how about we meditate on counsel? It is a unique gift that helps us speak the right words at appropriate times. We need the gift of counsel for ourselves. We also need it for others. It is a gift of service. How pleasant it can be for someone to say, "I like listening to you because your words edify and show the way in the dark."

Please also continue the novena prayer, "Veni Creator Spiritus."

REFLECT

O Holy Spirit, the love of the Father and the Son, you are called the Paraclete, one who is called in to defend or plead my cause. You do so not only by speaking the right words in the best possible way but by coming in at the right time. You never let me down.

You plead my cause, like the Son, against all condemnatory accusations from the enemy of my salvation. You come in to remedy a crumbling situation by the force of your presence and love. Your presence alone is consoling and revitalizing.

You are the counsel, directing the Church through the thick and thin of turbulent times. I remember when our Lord and Savior encouraged us to be of good cheer, never anxious, because you will tell us what to say at the right time (see Matthew 10:19). Yes! I believe it. I know it's true.

I know too that Christ will continue to be glorified in the life of believers (see John 17:10–11) if you dwell with us as the Lord promised.

O Holy Spirit, help me with the gift of counsel. I need it not only for myself but also for my family, the Church, the community, and all around me. I believe that with this gift of counsel, I can offer sound advice to those desperately in need of it.

There are many in need of spiritual and emotional support. How can I help if your grace of counsel isn't with me? I need this gift, Lord.

I need, too, to be blessed by counseling words in my down moments. The saying quoted by our Lord, "Doctor, cure yourself," is correct. All my life, I have not seen one who was the best counselor of him or herself. Second opinions—reasonable, holy, and appropriate counselors—are also needed.

During the time I need them most, may I receive from you good voices that inspire me. Let those who come in to say that word, beam that smile, or extend a handshake that is consoling, strengthening, and enlightening, flow from you.

May there also be more such people in this dark, confused world. May your Church be blessed with more and more ministers who hear your counsel and consolation. Holy Spirit, I don't even know what I am saying. However, I know and believe you hear the groans of my heart.

PRAY

Come, Holy Spirit. I need you. We need you. Speak your word of direction when we are at a crossroads. Amen.

Wednesday

Pentecost Novena, Day Six

Readings: Acts 20:28–38; John 17:11b–19

I welcome you to day six of the preparation to celebrate the coming of the Holy Spirit. I wonder what the disciples of Jesus must have been doing in the Upper Room during the sixth day of their prayers. Perhaps fatigue was already setting in since they had been fasting, living on bread and water alone, or something like that. Plus, they were living under the fear of the public opposed to their message, secluded and hiding in the Upper Room.

Are you getting tired? Try not to be, because the better part of the promise is yet to come. As the saying goes, "When the night is darkest, the dawn is near." The dawn of the Holy Spirit's coming is underway or, should I say, is near. Courage!

Today's prayerful meditation to the Holy Spirit is on courage, what we know in traditional spirituality as the gift of fortitude. It is the gift that gives us the strength to overcome fear so that we can courageously do God's will and live a life of joyful freedom.

I understand there are many reasons to be afraid. Many things scare us. It is in our nature to be frightened by certain situations.

Remember the time you came close to fire? Instinctively, your body shivered. Or that time something was thrown at you? The instinct of self-preservation, motivated by natural fear, took over and you ducked.

Many times, we are afraid to take up challenging tasks. We don't want to take risks because risks are often uncomfortable. How about spiritual adventures? Growth in spiritual life entails embracing spiritual adventures. Those who are courageous enough to take risks experience greatness and achieve their potential. The saints are courageous people.

However, we can't cultivate spiritual courage without the grace of God. It is a gift. It is God's gift, one of the gifts of the Holy Spirit. Thus, we need to ask for this gift.

In the prophecy of Zephaniah 3:16–18, we hear a message for Zion, a word applied to the Church as well. The message is about Emmanuel (Jesus Christ) dwelling with us, thereby being the source of our courage, strength, and victory. Christ's continuous presence in our midst is through his Spirit, the Holy Spirit. Being open and attuned to him is a spiritual bulwark.

Remember to continue the novena prayer, "Veni Creator Spiritus."

REFLECT

Oh, Holy Spirit, I know I lack courage. Yes, I receive good counsel, and I have a wealth of knowledge of what to do for your glory and the blessing of my neighbor, but I lack the courage to execute.

Many times I start something but lack the perseverance to follow through to the end. Similar to the parable told by our Lord Jesus Christ, I am like that man who starts a house or begins a project but can't finish. I hate it. I want to do it over. Yet I make the same mistakes again and again.

I need courage. I need endurance and perseverance. I need integrity of character so that my "Yes" will mean "Yes" and my "No" will mean "No." I need behavioral credibility. I don't want to swing from one position to another simply because I lack the courage to stand by what I know, what my mind is telling me is the right thing to do.

When I review the early Church's life, I realize that those people, especially the disciples, lock themselves in the Upper

Room because of fear. However, when you come upon them, they break the shackles of fear and courageously testify to what they know.

Give me the same courage. I should lead a life of freedom, confident about myself, rather than live a lie to please others.

PRAY

O Holy Spirit, fill my heart with the same Spirit of courage you gave the disciples. Strengthen my will to long for what is right and good, true and beautiful to you, for my neighbor and for me. Amen.

Thursday

Pentecost Novena, Day Seven

Readings: Acts 22:30; 23:6–11; John 17:20–26

*A*re you gradually settling in the right disposition to welcome the Holy Spirit? Recall I said at the beginning that this demands trust, the obedience of faith, and expectant faith. Our Lord Jesus has promised the Spirit and asks us, as the Church, to expect his renewing presence. That expectation flows from a spirit of piety.

Piety describes a gift that makes a heart aligned all the time to godliness. Such a soul is pure, like that of a child, and sees things from God's perspective. It is a disposition of holiness. Anyone whose heart is of that quality is totally in love with God. At the core of piety is love as strong as death. We do not create this love; the Holy Spirit grants it. In the classical spiritual theology of the Church from the scholastics, piety is a virtue of religion and reverence for holy things.

The Lord Jesus' long prayer in John 17 called the "Priestly Prayer of Jesus" shows how much he loves us and has willed that his love abide with us: "I made known to them thy name, and I will make it known, that the love with which thou hast loved me may be in them, and I in them" (John 17:26).

Don't you realize that the Church regards the Holy Spirit as the love between God the Father and God the Son? Thus, when the Spirit fills our hearts, we are wrapped in that love that is beyond all telling.

Saint Augustine, quoting Saint Paul, remarked, "The Holy Spirit pours the love of God in our hearts." The poured love manifests in different ways. It is on our faces, in our hands, in our gestures, and in our worship. It is in our relationships, indeed, in our thoughts and actions. Everything expresses that godliness, that love of God. It also manifests in piety. Don't you need this kind of love and devotion? I do.

Please continue the novena prayer, "Veni Creator Spiritus."

REFLECT

O Holy Spirit, many times, the things of the world sap me of that constant awareness of God's presence. I slip. Sadly, I backslide. I become so worldly in my thoughts, words, and actions that I fail to perceive you, to feel your holy hands holding me, your voice speaking to me, and your wings carrying me. I am so engrossed in my will and control of situations that I elbow you out of the plan.

Holy Spirit, please give me the gift of holy innocence as from the holy face of the infant Jesus so that nothing will make me lose sight of your aroma of love ingrained in everything around me.

Vacuum all the dirt from my spiritual senses so that I can enjoy the pleasant aroma of your presence around me. By so doing, I will loathe the repugnant smell of things that do not give you glory. May my spiritual senses be so pure that sin will be awful and distasteful. Like nectar, may my aspirations be drawn to those things that give you glory and bring joy, peace, and love to your people. Amen.

May I also have deep awe of the Lord knowing that he is God and I am his creature. May the privilege of his adoption of me in Christ not cause me to disrespect him but to respond in pious gratitude. Amen.

PRAY

O, Holy Spirit, come and make my heart like that of a child— pure, simple, and holy. Amen.

Friday

Pentecost Novena, Day Eight

Readings: Acts 25:13b–21; John 21:15–19

I welcome you to day eight of our devotional to the Holy Spirit. I have been talking about gifts, traditional gifts of the Holy Spirit. Let us not suppose that those are all that the Holy Spirit can give. In the storehouse of the Lord, there are uncountable gifts. Whatever is good, whatever is pleasant, name it; it is in God's gift bag.

Who does not want more gifts? I do. You know how you feel during festive times such as anniversaries, birthdays, and so on. People give you gifts. Always refreshing, isn't it? Not receiving gifts or a card at parties is discouraging. I tell you, the Holy Spirit isn't a no show. He never fails to give a gift. He is always present, always giving more gifts.

In reality, his gifts are designed, customized, personalized, and targeted for each individual for the common good and service (see 1 Corinthians 12:7; 1 Peter 4:10).

Thus we call those other, additional gifts, charisms or charisma. There are charisms for administration and leadership in the Church and society. There are different sorts of charisms for vocational calls and yet other charisms for building up the community's faith.

Those called and ordained as leaders of God's people receive the Holy Spirit charisms of administration, of hierarchy, as it is called. This is a unique charism of Church leadership. Paul's conversion and consequent commissioning (see Acts 9:1–20) is a clear example of this gift of leadership and service in the Church. We call this gift holy orders. Through holy orders, the food of angels, the Body and Blood of Jesus Christ, a necessary aspect of new life in Christ (see John 6:52–69), is made available to the faithful.

Those called for unique missions within the religious life or other distinctive communities receive a unique charism too, which is the spirituality of that congregation. It is what makes it different from others. You know the Holy Spirit is boundless in what he can give.

There are also charismatic gifts. These are without boundaries among the clergy, religious, and laity. They do not depend on whether you are clergy or laity. For instance, Saint Paul gives examples of those charismatic (spiritual) gifts in 1 Corinthians 12 and 13. His list does not exhaust what the Holy Spirit can provide to individuals. The list is endless because the Holy Spirit gives as the need arises.

When you receive these charisms, embrace and use them. There is no need to be shy about what you have or to be arrogant about it.

Use them responsibly and do not hinder the work of the Spirit. I know my gifts, and I am proud to use them for the gospel and service. There is freedom and joy in doing so. I hope you are proud of who you are in God and the gifts you have or will receive.

Continue the novena prayer, "Veni Creator Spiritus."

REFLECT

O Holy Spirit, I understand that in your storehouse of blessings, you have more than enough gifts to give me. They are gifts appropriate for my unique mission in life.

Unfortunately, I do not adequately understand how your gifts work or how to use them for service. I see my friends who manifest these gifts, but I erroneously think I don't have any. Even if I have gifts, I am not sure what they are. I need discernment to discover my gifts.

Besides, you know what gifts fit me and what will bring me closer to you and build up my family, the Church, and my community. Give me such gifts. I don't want to mention which ones, because I believe that since you are all-knowing, you certainly know the gifts appropriate for me and what you want me to do.

Above all, you know that many times my mind is fixed on what I want or what I think I need, which may not necessarily be what you know I need. Since no gifts can come to me unless I open my hands to accept them, give me the grace of proper disposition to accept your gifts.

PRAY

O Holy Spirit, let me not be a stumbling block to your generosity. May my will be attuned to what you are doing. Do not let prejudices due to abuses in the past from me, from others, or even from your Church make me unwilling to let you into my life. I pray for the grace of openness to your anointing grace. Amen.

Saturday

Pentecost Novena, Day Nine

Readings: Acts 28:16–20, 30–31; John 21:20–25

On this last day before the Sunday of Pentecost, let's reflect on gratitude as a beautiful response to gifts.

Gratitude is a necessary expectation upon giving a gift or gifts. There are many ways people say thank you, such as through cards, text messages, emails, emojis, and so on. Others reciprocate with a gift to the giver while others give back through service. In so doing, the line of mutual gift giving continues.

The story of the raising of Tabitha (Dorcas) from death by Saint Peter (see Acts 9:31–42) is an example of how a generous heart that gives receives life in return. Giving back is a gesture of gratitude.

Lack of gratitude can be the death of gift giving and goodwill. You know how it feels when you spend time getting a gift for somebody and the person does not say thank you or is less than sincere. It hurts, doesn't it?

Let's not think it hurts the Holy Spirit if we do not reciprocate his gifts. What it does is disconnect us from the constant flow of gifts.

See what I mean by understanding what "Thank you" or gratitude means to the Holy Spirit. The coming of the Holy Spirit is intended to strengthen and empower us to bear witness to Christ. All the gifts enhance this central mission. The gifts are, therefore, an instrument for promoting the kingdom of God, which is grace and mercy through salvation in Christ, leading to the forming of the community of faith as the family of salvation. Hence, the receiver appreciates the gifts when they are used for the reason they have been given. This is Gratitude 101.

Using gifts for the reason God gives them builds the community. In turn, the giver, the Holy Spirit, strengthens and renews us and we begin to bear much fruit. Hence, we have the fruits of the Holy Spirit.

The phrase "fruits of the Spirit" expresses the life of gratitude people feel when they receive the gifts of the Holy Spirit. Fruits such as love, joy, peace, patience, kindness, goodness, faithfulness, and purity as Saint Paul lists in Galatians 5:22–23 build us. They manifest in a life of gratitude to God for all he has done for us. Fruits of the Holy Spirit enhance our spiritual growth as individuals.

Therefore, a true novena to the Holy Spirit builds us in such a way as to bear fruits. In part, these fruits, God's gifts and grace and our response to these gifts, truly make us more like God. Or, rather, they make us God's special people, those living the life led by the Holy Spirit.

Please continue the novena prayer, "Veni Creator Spiritus."

REFLECT

Holy Spirit, as we come to the last day awaiting your renewing presence, remind me of the need to bear fruit or, should I say, to harvest the fruit you give. I mean the fruit of joy so that my life will be that of joy, the fruit of love that I love as you love.

I need the fruit of happiness and peace so that I will be a steadfast instrument of peace and so that nothing will make me so sad as to lose hope and joy.

Grant me the fruit of kindness and mercy so that others will see in me the heart of God's kindness.

Bless me with the fruit of forgiveness so that I will no longer hold on to hurts and will instead be free and set people free from hurts.

I also ask for the fruit of truthfulness so that I will stamp out lies from all that I do and say.

Make me live with such gratitude that everything I do will glorify you, the Father and the Son. Amen.

PRAY

O Holy Spirit, welcome into my heart. Make me an instrument of your love and grace. Use me. Lead me. Inspire me. Amen. May my life be a big thank you to the Father, the Son, and the Holy Spirit. May my life mirror you in the community in which I live and work. Amen.

Pentecost Sunday

Come Holy Spirit, Enkindle in Us the Fire of Love

Readings, Year A: Acts 2:1–11; Corinthians 12:3b–7, 12–13

Reading, Year B: Galatians 5:16–25

Alternative Reading, Year B: John 20:19–23

Second Alternative Readings, Year B: John 15:26–27; 16:12–15

Reading, Year C: Romans 8:8–17

Alternative Readings, Year C: John 14:15–16, 23b–26

Permit me to begin today's reflection with a famous story told by the Greek philosopher, Plutarch, about a renowned geometrician. At the peak of the discovery of the science of mathematics, a prominent geometrician of the Pythagorean school bragged of his ability to make any figure, no matter how crooked or twisted, stand at an upright position. All it took, he claimed, was getting the proper right angle combination (90 degrees) and harmonizing it with gravity. He achieved much success in doing this until one day when a smart student challenged him to make a corpse stand erect.

The great geometrician did not see any difficulty in doing this. He started by trying various balancing schemes, experimenting with different postures, and exploring all possible combinations of angles that, under normal circumstances, should give 90 degrees and therefore make the dead body stand erect. He compassed, for example, 45/45, 50/40, 89/1, 70/20, but it was all a failure. He tried again and again, to no avail. At last, he threw in the towel with the exclamation, "I do not know what is wrong with this figure; there seems to be something missing on the inside."

The acknowledgment of this geometrician and his submission of his limitations are didactic. Imagine a human being without a soul—that spiritual principle that is the subject of our consciousness and freedom. It is unthinkable, because, without the soul, all we see is a dead body. Hence, even one of the greatest mathematicians of ancient times couldn't put "life" in the dead body. The dead can't stand on their own. Only those alive can stand, walk, choose, and act. We can become the best we are called to be on Earth and, as the psalmist says, "praise God" because we are alive to do so.

The French spiritual writer Dom Jean-Baptiste Chautard (1858–1935) in the classic book *The Soul of the Apostolate* invites us to take the interior life, the life of the spirit, seriously. He is alluding to the presence of the Spirit of Christ, the Holy Spirit, in the Church. The Holy Spirit is the "soul of the apostolate" for good reason. Through the Holy Spirit, Christ, with God the Father, continues to abide in the Church. One can't imagine a church not being led by the Holy Spirit.

The Holy Spirit comes on the day of Pentecost to commission the Church and all members of the Church to become "missionary disciples," using the phrase of Pope Francis. Thus, we become witnesses of the risen Lord to all. Hence, on Pentecost Day, the Church is born, a Church whose primary vocation on Earth is to evangelize. As Pope Paul VI emphasized, "Evangelizing is, in fact, the grace and vocation proper to the Church, her deepest identity."[12]

The Holy Spirit is the sole animator of the Church, the soul of virtuous spiritual life. Today, we celebrate that memorable birthday of

---

12. Pope Paul VI, Apostolic Exhortation *Evangelii Nuntiandi* (Vatican City: December 8, 1975), no. 14.

the Church on Pentecost. For my reflection on the significance of the Pentecost, please read the reflection following this one.

At Pentecost, souls dead in sin are revived, a new encounter that makes us stand upright as disciples of Jesus Christ starts. At Pentecost, a timid person like Peter who denies Jesus three times when his courageous confession is most needed (see John 18:25–27) becomes a bold preacher before a multitude. The Holy Spirit breaks the barriers of fear, insecurity, and cowardice.

At Pentecost, a withdrawn, insecure, and shy apostolic community locked in the Upper Room (Acts 1:13ff) stands in eloquence. They speak in tongues and testify boldly about the wonders of the risen Lord. They become evangelizers (Acts 2ff). The Holy Spirit makes the Church a bold vanguard of the truth and makes believers audacious emissaries of the Good News.

At Pentecost, there are miracles, healings, and deliverance. In the same way, the Holy Spirit goes on to provide signs and wonders for those who welcome him: "Taste and see that the Lord is good."

At Pentecost, the fire of love is kindled (see Acts 2:3). The Holy Spirit shatters the shackles of hatred, exploitation, and unholy relationships and promotes genuine love among people. Pure love for God and one another is by the Holy Spirit.

At Pentecost, the community is bonded in love, obedience, and eagerness to relive the Christ experience, overturning the reality of the Tower of Babel. No better explanation is given that men and women from different tongues and nations speak one language of love, live in love, share from the same cup, and participate at the same table in the Eucharist if not for the bonding impact of the Holy Spirit.

The Holy Spirit-led Church is a church wherein space, locality, or structures are not barriers. Rather, all become vehicles of orderliness through which the unity of faith and the bond of love blossom. As the psalmist says, it is like olive branches around the table of the Lord (see Psalms 128:3).

REFLECT

Do I know the Holy Spirit's role in the life of the Church and my life as a believer? What is the relevance of the celebration of Pentecost in my life?

PRAY

Come, Holy Spirit, and fill the hearts of the faithful. Enkindle in us the fire of your love. Amen.

Alternative Reflection

Welcome Holy Spirit—Exploring the Meaning and Significance of the Coming of the Holy Spirit on Pentecost Day

Readings, Year A: Acts 2:1–11; Corinthians 12:3b–7, 12–13

Reading, Year B: Galatians 5:16–25

Alternative Reading, Year B: John 20:19–23

Second Alternative Readings, Year B: John 15:26–27; 16:12–15

Reading, Year C: Romans 8:8–17

Alternative Readings, Year C: John 14:15–16, 23b–26

With God, there is no accident. Coincidence, luck, and chance have no place in the divine plan. Every plan of God is providence. In other words, providence is another way of speaking about the divine plan.

It is providence that the finger of God directs things from the start to their final fulfillment. As the Catholic Catechism says, God has set things *in statu via*, "in a state of journeying" towards realizing the ultimate plan.[13]

It is providence that we have day and night. It is providence that we have seasons—summer, winter, spring, or autumn, and for those in sub-Saharan Africa, the rainy season, dry season, and harmattan season.

---

13. See *Catechism of the Catholic Church*, no. 302.

It is providence that we have people of different colors and languages. The sequence of birth, growth, and death is providence. Things happen by providence.

Among the histories of the world's peoples, we see this narrative of providence in different ways. The history of the people of Israel is a perfect case study.

It is providence that God creates the first man and woman. It is providence that God calls Abram (Abraham) from the land of Ur to be a pacesetter for human response to the true God. Abraham's story is providence at work.

It is providence that the sons of Israel go to Egypt. God is already preparing a way through Joseph, second of the last of Israel's twelve sons, to make way for his brothers. It is also providence that they move to Egypt. Then comes the persecution by Pharaoh, and God redeems them by his right hand and arm outstretched.

The entire event of the Passover is providence: "When I see the blood, I will pass over you" (see Exodus 12:13). Passover is designed in preparation for reconfiguring God's people to the original holiness lost by the sins of our first parents. Freedom from Egypt prefigures deliverance from the clutches of sin, no thanks to Original Sin, which the Lamb, Our Lord Jesus Christ, objectively accomplishes on Good Friday.

In other words, all three major feasts that God asks the people of Israel to celebrate are part of a providential plan. They are all *in statu via*—a process towards fulfillment.

Permit me to refresh our minds on the three major feasts and to show some parallels with our Christian Faith. First is the Passover, the Feast of Unleavened Bread (Thanksgiving). It's a weeklong feast of thanksgiving to God for delivering Israel from the hand of Pharaoh, the king of Egypt. Our Church sees this feast as finding its ultimate fulfillment at the Crucifixion of Jesus Christ, the true and worthy Lamb of God, who takes away the sins of the world.

During the actual Jewish Passover, people drink from the chalice and eat the bread. The cup of salvation, especially the fourth cup, is the consummation of the Lamb's blood, poured for the salvation of the world. Christ fulfills that process on Good Friday. Providentially, Jesus' crucifixion happens on or around the Passover. In every Church that celebrates the Eucharist as the body and blood of Jesus, the Passover is reenacted. Passover, once consummated, is memorialized (see Matthew 26:17–30). This is providence.

The second Jewish feast is the Feast of the Shavuot (Pentecost). It's also called the Feast of Weeks (see Exodus 34:22) or the Feast of Harvest or Firstfruits (Numbers 28:26). This feast is celebrated on the day they harvest the first fruit of the land. Equally, it symbolizes the birth of their nationhood as a fruitful nation in the land flowing with milk and honey whose constitution is the Law of God. The locus of the congregation is Mount Sinai, where God gives Moses the Torah and his wind, breath, or Spirit thunders. This feast is celebrated fifty days after the Passover.

Our Christian Passover is Good Friday, and the Resurrection is Easter. Approximately fifty days after, the Holy Spirit descends on the disciples, on the very day of harvest celebration. It is the day the Jews celebrate as the birthday of their nationhood and the receiving of the Torah (meaning five books). It is also the day regarded as the Harvest of Fruitfulness.

On the first Pentecost, about three thousand people were slain because of the people's idolatry in worshiping the golden calf (see Exodus 32:28). On the first Christian Pentecost, about three thousand people become believers after listening to the first spirit-filled sermon of Saint Peter (see Acts 2:41). A new day of grace for God's people has dawned. This is providence.

Therefore, Pentecost is a day of Thanksgiving for God's grace of fruitfulness to his people. For us, it is providence that on that day, the Church is born as a people filled with the Spirit of the Father and the Son. The Church is to be fruitful in begetting sons and daughters for the Lord.

On this day, as in the promise of the Old Testament, we receive God's love, no longer on a tablet of stone but in our hearts. God's love is poured into our hearts through his Spirit. This is technically the day of the first fruit of the Lamb. This is providence. I will get back to this, but for now, let's sketch the last Jewish feast.

The third and last major Jewish feast is the Feast of Tabernacles. It is the feast in remembrance of the end of the long journey, of Israel's wandering in the wilderness. It is a weeklong celebration called the *eschaton* (that is, given the final restoration and covenant with the Lord as suggested by Zechariah 14 and Ezekiel 43:27). A Christian parallel of this feast sees it as yet to be fulfilled. It will occur when the Church Pilgrim, also called the Church Militant, will end our journey on Earth and witness the beatific vision. This is divine providence as well.

But back to the Pentecost. If we see the historical, providential connections between the Jewish Feast of Pentecost and the Christian Feast of the Coming of the Holy Spirit on the day of Pentecost, we can be inspired to see the bigger picture of the divine plan.

On the day of Pentecost, the Holy Spirit descends on the disciples like tongues of fire. The Spirit gives them utterances—they prophesy, speak boldly of what they have seen, heard, touched, tasted, and felt in Christ. The coming of the Holy Spirit is God's plan, God's promise fulfilled. They welcome him, the person through whom the Church's fruitfulness is born. As the Church, they speak in varied tongues but one language—the language of love because the Holy Spirit is love.

As we open our hearts to the gripping and transforming presence of the Third Person of the Trinity, the Holy Spirit, let us reconnect with this divine plan. Be part of this plan and consciously choose to celebrate, especially at the Eucharist. The celebration connected with the Passover guarantees a visit by the Spirit of the Lamb of the Pasch—the Holy Spirit. No one who consciously, actively connects with God's plan goes home unfulfilled.

> **REFLECT**
> How can I show gratitude to God for the grace of his providence in sending us the Holy Spirit?
>
> **PRAY**
> I welcome you, Holy Spirit. Make my heart a home for you. Amen.

A Day after Pentecost

Memorial of Mary, the Mother of the Church—Behold Your Mother

Readings: Genesis 3:9–15, 20 or Acts 1:12–14; John 19:25–34

*A*fter yesterday's Pentecost Sunday celebration, we're back to the ordinary time of the year. I hope you are invigorated to continue living the life of Christ and bearing witness to the Good News of his saving grace.

Today we celebrate the memorial of Mary, the mother of the Church. It is the newest feast of the Blessed Virgin Mary decreed by the Holy Father Pope Francis in 2018. The holy father authorized that it be included in the Catholic Roman Calendar, Missal, and Divine Office. We celebrate it on the first day after Pentecost Sunday. Cardinal Robert Sarah, Prefect of the Congregation for Divine Worship and Discipline of the Sacraments, published the news on March 3, 2018.

We celebrate Mary as the mother of the Church. She is our mother because Jesus is our brother. Also, as the mother of Our Lord, Savior, and God, Jesus Christ, she is our mother too. I am not shy to call the precious woman who bore me my mom. I also don't feel shy to call the woman who has adopted me as her son in the United States my mom too. I'm certainly not shy to call Mary, the mother of my Lord and Savior, my mother. The Blessed Virgin Mary is my most beloved mom, and I am proud to tell it to the mountains.

As a believer in the Lord Jesus Christ, I count myself among the beloved of the Lord. I see myself as John, the beloved. I see myself like that apostle whom the Lord loved so much. I hope you, as a believer in the Lord and Savior Jesus Christ, see yourself that way.

A particular quotation comes to mind as I reflect on this privilege of seeing myself as a beloved child of God. It is that description regarding the love of Jesus for all believers. The Gospel of John writes that Jesus loves his own in the world to the end (see John 13:1). We read all through Scripture how much Jesus loves us.

We are among those the Lord chooses in accord with his richness. Scripture says he chooses us in him before the foundation of the world (see Ephesians 1:4).

What the Lord Jesus does at the foot of the cross, as reported in the Gospel of John, is precious to me and to my faith life. He looks down as if from heaven and sees Mary, his mother, and the disciple he loves standing near. He says to his mother, "Woman, behold, your son." Then to the beloved disciple he says, "Behold, your mother" (John 19:26–27). Right there, the Lord gives a special gift to the people he died to save. That gift is his mom. He gives her, in particular, to all the beloved, to those who are his disciples.

Why does Scripture write about this event describing John the beloved as the "loved disciple"? Why doesn't the inspired writer use other adjectives such as the "loved apostle" as was common in many other parts of the gospel? Why also, in this scenario, does Jesus call Mary "Woman" instead of "Mother"?

Could it be that describing John as the beloved apostle in this setting suggests that the symbolism reserves Mary's motherhood only to the apostles? If so, then Mary's motherhood would belong to those whose roles are in the apostles' line, those in top church leadership—the bishops. One could make the claim that by using "disciple," the gospel wants us all as disciples and calls us all to be part of the Lord's mother's life since we are his brothers and sisters. The above analysis is how the text speaks to me.

The Lord calls his mom "woman" because this particular woman, Mary, is the fulfillment of the prophecies about the "new Eve." She is the woman Scripture says right from the beginning is the one through whose child redemption will be given to the world (see Genesis 3:15).

I take Mother Mary as my mother. She is the mother of the Church. She is the mother of our Lord and our mother too. She is that mother closest to the Lord and an integral part of the early Church. Her intimacy with the Lord as his mother from conception through his early life and maturity at the foot of the cross during the Resurrection and clearly at the Upper Room when the Church is born at the time the Holy Spirit descends on the disciples is self-evident.

In my personal spiritual life, Mother Mary does not fail me. Closeness to her has deepened my relationship with the Lord through grace. She has been an exceptional heavenly support in my work of prayers and evangelization. For instance, daily, I receive prayer petitions from people worldwide, asking for intercessions. I count this a privilege. However, I know I can do nothing to find answers to their needs. Only God can. So I take their petitions to God. I often find that many of those petitions that seem too difficult to crack are answered, miraculously, through Mother Mary. When I ask Mother Mary to carry those prayer points on my behalf to her Son and my Lord Jesus Christ, I receive incredible breakthroughs.

I salute Mother Mary with that greeting of the angel (Luke 1:28). I chant to her that song of the redeemed. When I do so, her Son, Jesus the Lord, is glorified because he sees in my heart the deep love for that mom through whom he chose to take flesh.

I cherish everything about the Blessed Virgin Mary because God delighted in her first. Who am I not to bless whom God has blessed among all women?

Mary, my mama and the mother of the Church, help me discover the tender love and grace of the Holy Spirit through whom you bore your Son, Jesus Christ, the Lord. As a mom, accompany me to know those hidden things about Jesus, those things about a child, that only moms know.

I love you, Mother Mary. I love and worship you, Jesus, my Lord and Savior.

REFLECT

As a believer in the Lord and Savior Jesus Christ, how is my relationship with the mother of my Lord? Do I treat her with the reverence deserved of the saintly mom? How do I appreciate her role in my redemption in Christ?

PRAY

Hail Mary, full of grace. The Lord is with you. Blessed are you among women and blessed is the fruit of your womb, Jesus. Holy Mary, mother of God, pray for us sinners, now and at the hour of death. Amen.

CONCLUSION

I hope you have found these reflections helpful in your spiritual life. If so, it would be a wonderful idea to pass them on to someone else who may benefit. Joy shared is joy multiplied. You will also benefit from volumes four to seven as each covers different aspects of the ordinary time and Sundays. Thanks for joining me in this prayerful journey.

God love you. God bless you.

Appendix

Veni, Creator Spiritus

In English

Come, Holy Spirit, Creator blest,
and in our souls take up Thy rest;
come with Thy grace and heavenly aid
to fill the hearts which Thou hast made.

O comforter, to Thee we cry,
O heavenly gift of God Most High,
O fount of life and fire of love,
and sweet anointing from above.

Thou in Thy sevenfold gifts are known;
Thou, finger of God's hand we own;
Thou, promise of the Father,
Thou Who dost the tongue with power imbue.

Kindle our sense from above,
and make our hearts o'erflow with love;
with patience firm and virtue high
the weakness of our flesh supply.

Far from us drive the foe we dread,
and grant us Thy peace instead;
so shall we not, with Thee for guide,
turn from the path of life aside.

Oh, may Thy grace on us bestow
the Father and the Son to know;
and Thee, through endless times confessed,
of both the eternal Spirit blest.

Now to the Father and the Son,
Who rose from death, be glory given,
with Thou, O Holy Comforter,
henceforth by all in earth and heaven. Amen.

In Latin

Veni, Creator Spiritus,
mentes tuorum visita,
imple superna gratia
quae tu creasti pectora.

Qui diceris Paraclitus,
altissima donum Dei,
fons vivus, ignis, caritas,
et spiritalis unctio.

Tu, septiformis munere,
digitus paternae dexterae,
Tu rite promissum Patris,
sermone ditans guttura.

Accende lumen sensibus:
infunde amorem cordibus:
infirma nostri corporis
virtute firmans perpeti.

Hostem repellas longius,
pacemque dones protinus:
ductore sic te praevio
vitemus omne noxium.

Per te sciamus da Patrem,
noscamus atque Filium;
Teque utrisque Spiritum
credamus omni tempore.

Deo Patri sit gloria,
et Filio, qui a mortuis
surrexit, ac Paraclito,
in saeculorum saecula.

Amen.

Other Resources for Your Daily Reflections and Devotionals

An Encounter Volumes I and II

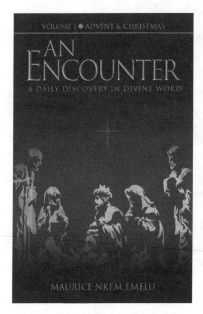 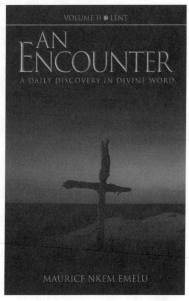

Available from booksellers, Amazon, Catholic bookstores, and the author's website, revemelu.com.

To share your thoughts and comments with the author, email info@revemelu.com.